The Road of Donkey Bones: A 1918 Diary from Britain's WW1 East Africa Campaign

Researched and compiled by Alison Cornell

Grosvenor House
Publishing Limited

All rights reserved
Copyright © Alison Cornell, 2020

The right of Alison Cornell to be identified as the author of this
work has been asserted in accordance with Section 78
of the Copyright, Designs and Patents Act 1988

The book cover is copyright to Alison Cornell

This book is published by
Grosvenor House Publishing Ltd
Link House
140 The Broadway, Tolworth, Surrey, KT6 7HT.
www.grosvenorhousepublishing.co.uk

This book is sold subject to the conditions that it shall not, by way of
trade or otherwise, be lent, resold, hired out or otherwise circulated
without the author's or publisher's prior consent in any form of binding or
cover other than that in which it is published and
without a similar condition including this condition being imposed
on the subsequent purchaser.

A CIP record for this book
is available from the British Library

ISBN 978-1-78623-651-7

*In memory of my father whom I loved dearly
and the father he never knew or had the opportunity to love dearly.*

*In memory also of over 1,000,000 African
soldiers, carriers and civilians who
lost their lives as a result of action to defend
our colonies between 1914 -1918 and whose
sacrifice, even 100 years on, is all too rarely
reported, acknowledged or honoured.*

The Dead

These hearts were woven of human joys and cares,
Washed marvellously with sorrow, swift to mirth.
The years had given them kindness. Dawn was theirs,
And sunset, and the colours of the earth.

These had seen movement, and heard music; known
Slumber and waking; loved; gone proudly friended;
Felt the quick stir of wonder; sat alone;
Touched flowers and furs and cheeks.
All this is ended.

There are waters blown by changing winds to laughter
And lit by the rich skies, all day. And after,
Frost, with a gesture, stays the waves that dance
And wandering loveliness. He leaves a white
Unbroken glory, a gathered radiance,
A width, a shining peace, under the night.

Rupert Brooke

Table of Contents

Foreword by Alison Cornell ix

Glossary of Terms xiv

PART I – 1896 – 1917 1

    I a. Family Background and Early Life 3

    I b. Military Service and Life 1914-1917 7

    I c. Medal Group 13

    I d. Diary and Photo Albums 15

    I e. 1917 photos from Albums 17

PART II – 1918 Diary - East Africa Campaign 21

    II a. January – March 1918 23

    II b. April – June 1918 79

    II c. July – October 1918 133

PART III – 1918 – 1922 159

    III a. Russia 161

    III b. Home Life & Territorial Army Unit 165

    III c. Death 169

    III d. Additional diary photographs 175

    III e. Advertisements from the diary 183

Appendices 185

References 209

Foreword

Llewellyn Wynne-Jones was my paternal grandfather. He died at the age of just 26 in 1921, so I never had the privilege to know him. He was known in the family as 'Wynne' so that is how I shall refer to him in this book.

My father (his son) Philip, never really knew his father. In a deeply tragic turn of events, Wynne died just two days before his only son's first birthday.

So many young men had died in the Great War, and then from the great flu pandemic, that for my father, growing up having only a mother was not unusual. He was luckier than many, being raised in financially secure circumstances, living with his mother Gwladys's family, the Nicholases of The Grange, Maesteg, Glamorgan. He was surrounded and much loved by his paternal relatives as well.

Gwladys was the eldest of Alfred and Hannah Nicholas's five children and their only girl. Having married in October 1917, she and Wynne were just setting out on their life together when he died. Her initial joy and relief at having her young husband home safe from the war and her excitement at their first child was to be so cruelly taken by his untimely death. Though I knew her extremely well as a child (she died in 1977) she never talked to me about this enormous loss, neither did she ever seem bitter. She was just a lovely grandma. Now of course, I so wish I had spoken to her about her husband and her early life.

Philip was raised to be aware of his father's service, but this was not a generation to show off. It was only when my family experienced a burglary in the 1970s that I really became aware of Wynne. I recall my father being particularly upset over the loss of a silver cigarette case with a dent from a bullet in it. It had been his fathers and of course credited with having saved his life on the Western Front. A talisman if you will, and as such much treasured by his son.

In 1982 my father gave me Wynne's 1918 war diary as I had always been interested in family history. The spidery writing is hard to decipher but I set to transcribing it by hand into an unused 1982 desk diary. This was long before computers were the norm of course, so the opportunities for research around the narrative were so much more limited than is the case today. The time I was able to give to it was also much more limited.

Along with the diary came four photo albums containing pictures which Wynne had taken during his service in the 1918 East Africa campaign.

At around this time, and probably with the burglary in mind, my father gave Wynne's medals to the Royal Welch Fusiliers Museum in Caernarvon. Although he knew I would treasure them, he never wanted them sold by future generations, or indeed taken by thieves. They remain on display at the Regimental Museum to this day.

RESEARCHED AND COMPILED BY ALISON CORNELL

When you show an interest in family history all manner of treasures are forwarded to you following the deaths of elderly relatives. So over the years I have collected a mini archive of family photos and documents. All too often these treasures had remained packed in boxes – it can be so hard to find the time to go through them.

In 2014 I found myself unexpectedly redundant and decided to look once again at the archive I had. The first thing that struck me was what an incredible life Wynne had. He achieved more in his meagre 26 years than most of us do in a lifetime. Humbling indeed. But what to do with all the information and documentation?

I began to organise, to scan documents, to put them in some kind of order and to try and piece together the family story.

In February 2017, while going through a file which had come from my Auntie Gina's house (Gina was one of Wynne's sisters) I came across a series of letters written by Wynne's younger brother, Hywel from the Western Front 100 years earlier. (Appendix 1)

A young 19 year old boy writing home with such enthusiasm; wanting to 'do his bit' for King and Country and 'fight the Hun'. Youthful enthusiasm and patriotic naiveite spill from the pages of Hywel's letters.

With his older brother having been awarded the Military Cross just a year earlier, it is clear that young Hywel, like so many brave young men of his generation, was anxious to serve his country and prove his worth. He was blindly patriotic and utterly determined to make his family and friends proud.

I read the letters with a sombre sense of tragedy and the dread of impending loss. Hywel was so young and so innocent. I know he was not unusual in that, but his writing really bought home the tragedy of his generation. He was but a boy, not yet a man. He knew not what he faced, but his enthusiastic and patriotic words bounced up from the paper as though from the pages of a Boys Own annual.

Hywel Jones – c 1916

Hywel Jones grave – 2017

The last letter in this collection was in a different hand. It was written by Private J W Daley and was a report on the circumstances of Hywel's death on 4 March 1917.

While inspecting the men in the trenches, he walked past an ammunition store just as it was hit by a stray shell blowing up Hywel and his servant, both of whom died shortly afterwards. Tragically Hywel barely got a chance to serve before his life was so pointlessly ended.

As I read these letters, I realised that the 100th anniversary of Hywel's death was just five days away. I was fairly certain that no one from the family had ever visited his grave. They probably never had the money.

I had all the information about his burial. His original resting place having been just behind the lines at Clery Sur Somme where he fell. These 'temporary' graves were often cleared by the War Graves Commission after the war and so Hywel's body was exhumed and reinterred, finally resting with his comrades at Perrone Communal Cemetery Extension.

And so it was that I decided to visit his grave on the 4 March 2017, the 100th anniversary of his death. His father's portrait has hung in my hall for years and I wanted to honour his son 100 years on. It was a wet Saturday when I drove, via the tunnel, to pay my respects, remember Hywel and plant a small daffodil bulb to honour his Welsh heritage, and I'm so glad I did. As anyone who has visited war graves will know, it is both a shocking and a humbling experience. The extent of these beautifully kept repositories for the lives of a generation is beyond imagining.

Llewellyn Wynne Jones – c 1917

As the centenary of the end of the Great War approached, I decided I should also do something to commemorate the life of my grandfather, Wynne, but the question was, what? And then it struck me, his diary and photographs could be shared as an act of remembrance. I decided it would be interesting to set up a Facebook page and post a page a day from his 1918 diary in order to follow his experiences 100 years on. The posts would be illustrated with many of the photos from his personal albums.

On 2 January 2018 I began my post which soon attracted considerable interest from family, fusiliers, historians and others from all over the world.

'Living' with grandfather day by day 100 years on proved to be a more personal and emotional experience than I had imagined. As time went on, I became more absorbed in trying to identify the places he had been and the things he had seen. The availability of resources on the internet has been a game changer in allowing me to "see" some of the places grandfather went, some of the ships he sailed on and some of the experiences he had. As the year went on, I found myself increasingly educated about WW1 in Africa. I read a great deal around the subject and became somewhat absorbed in this almost secret history. Not all of that information could be posted on Facebook, but I did want to bring it all together in one place.

The sacrifices of the Great War generation are literally unimaginable to us today. Yet we must imagine, we must remember – not just to honour all those who paid the ultimate price but for ourselves. This is where political failure, blind loyalty and misplaced passion can lead. This is what it can do. The sacrifices affected all who lived, loved and lost in 1914-18; parents, siblings, children, wives, friends, and comrades alike. Only through remembering can we even hope to prevent such atrocities, such sins against our common humanity from ever happening again.

Of course, we all know that though men like Wynne called WW1 'the war to end all wars' just 21 years later, barely a generation, the world would find itself at war once again. Many children whose fathers had either made the ultimate sacrifice or fought so bravely for King and Country in 1914-18 faced the same challenge in their late teens and early twenties.

In publishing this diary, I also hope to raise awareness of the more than 1,000,000 African soldiers, carriers and civilians who died in WW1 and to honour the enormous sacrifice they made. The impact of the East Africa campaign is still felt today on that great continent. Though often thought of as some kind of side show compared to the war in Europe, WW1 in Africa was anything but. In some districts of Africa up to 20% of their menfolk were killed; Kenya lost 13% of its entire male population. Simply staggering.

Britain spent £70 million on the East Africa campaign - close to the entire war budget for 1914. The scale of the war's losses prompted a previously unimagined pressure for remembrance, but it was many years before the sacrifices made in Africa would be commemorated. One Colonial Office official wrote at the time that the only reason it had not become a scandal was *"... because the people who suffered most were the carriers - and after all, who cares about native carriers?"*

In all the centenary commemorations I have seen since 2014, this East Africa Campaign remains hugely underrepresented. I owe much of my knowledge to the excellent book 'Tip & Run' by Edward Paice[1] which sets out in detail the entirety of the war in East Africa. For those in any doubt, I would simply say read this book.

The fighting was fierce and brutal, the sacrifice enormous and comparable to much of what happened in Europe and the daily adversities faced led some soldiers writing home to compare it unfavourably with their experience on the Western Front.

These soldiers faced all manner of privations; the local wildlife including lions, crocodiles, mosquitoes, snakes, hippopotami; the weather conditions with extreme heat, extreme rain, humidity; the geography with endless long marches across impossible, often barely charted terrain, from jungles to deserts, mountains to crocodile infested swamps, frequently with little or no water or supplies. There was no village "behind the lines" to have some down time between stints in the trenches as on the western front. They were in the middle of nowhere. It was pitiless.

I hope that this account of my grandfather's part in this brutal campaign provides some further opportunity to remember and honour the sacrifices made by those brave men. I have found it hard not to view it's continued under representation in our collective remembrance as a form of racism. That might have been unsurprising in 1918, that it continues in 2018 is perhaps as tragic as the war itself.

In his all too brief 26 years my grandfather was born in Nevis, educated in Honiton, Devon, took his Bar exams in Canada, fought with distinction in France, Africa and Russia, receiving the Military Cross and Bar, set up a Territorial Army Unit in Maesteg, married, had a son, completed his bar exams and began to establish his practice as a Barrister at law on the South Wales circuit.

Most of us don't achieve that much with three times as many years. Wynne's was clearly a life about quality not quantity which makes his loss our loss and all the more tragic.

What might he have achieved with his three score years and ten?

He surely deserves to be remembered and it has been my privilege to be part of that.

Alison Cornell – 2019

GLOSSARY of Acronyms and Abbreviations

A.A.G.	-	Assistant Adjutant General
B.E.A.	-	British East Africa
G.E.A.	-	German East Africa
K.A.R.	-	Kings African Rifles
M.C.	-	Military Cross
M.G.	-	Machine Gunner
M.I.	-	Military Intelligence
M.O.	-	Medical Officer
N.C.O.	-	Non Commissioned Officer
P.O.	-	Political Officer
P.O.E.A.	-	Political Officer East Africa
R.A.M.C.	-	Royal Army Medical Corps
S.M.O.	-	Senior Medical Officer
Q.M.S.	-	Quartermaster Sergeant
B.E.F.	-	British Expeditionary Force

There are several occasions in this book where language which today we quite rightly class as offensive is used. In particular the 'n' word. My apologies for any offense caused, however, it is the language of its time and I believe it is more honest to keep it in rather than 'asterix' it.

Throughout this book, where photographs from Wynne's albums are included and they have a label accompanying them, that label is exactly what Wynne had written either on the back of the photograph or underneath it in the album. Many, of course, have no such annotation.

PART 1

1896 - 1917

I a. Family Background and Early Life

My grandfather, Llewellyn Wynne Jones was born on the caribean island of Nevis in or around February 1896. He was baptised in the parish of St Georges, in the diocese of Antigua on 11th February 1896.

The Jones Family Nevis – c 1896/7

This remarkable photograph shows the Jones family and their house servants on Nevis with (from left to right) Wynne as a baby on his nannys lap, two further servants, Reverand John Jones, Mary Jones with children John, Gina and Annie in the front row. I have no information about the servants, but it is lovely to see them included here in the photo.

Wynne's parents John and Mary Jones had married at St Thomas' Church in Lambeth, London on 4th October 1883 when John was working as a schoolmaster in the area. Both came originally from the Ammanfod area of South Wales.

In 1884 John Jones took what must surely have been a momentous decision to move the family out to Nevis and St Kitts in the West Indies. Their first child, Gina, was just nine months old. John took up a post as schoolmaster on the island of St Kitts. Later that year he took holy orders being ordained as a preist by the Bishop of Anigua and serving as Rector of St George and St John on the neighbouring island of Nevis.

Unlike his older sisters Annie and Gina, Wynne would not have remembered much of life on Nevis as he was barely two when the family returned to the UK. None the less, he would have had a sense of the world and it's possibilities which not every young Welsh boy would have had at the turn of the last century.

The commemorative plaque which Gina had placed in Nevis

Beautiful as Nevis undoubtedly was, island life was not without it's hardships for the Jones family. In their eight years there as the 19th century drew to a close, four of their children were lost in infancy.

When my Auntie Gina died in 1982, amongst her effects was a group of envelopes containing locks of hair from those lost children. She had kept them safely all those years and yet in life, though I knew her well, she never spoke of them.

In the 1980s my Aunty Gina arranged for a plaque to be placed in the church on Nevis commemorating her long lost siblings. In an interview she did with BBC Radio Medway in 1980 (Appendix 2) at the age of 96 she barely mentioned these children.

Her sister Annie's love for and memories of the West Indies are rather beautifully referenced in a poem I found amongst Gina's effects (Appendix 3). I know not who it was from, it is signed simply W.P. but it speaks to a longing for that beauty and perhaps for someone with whom to share it.

Annie and Gina's generation lost so many loved ones. The combination of war and spanish flu having so depleted the population, particularly of males, neither Annie nor Gina would ever marry, and yet both lived full and exciting lives with no obvious signs of bitterness or negativity.

They were both wonderful aunts to their lost brother's only child and to his children.

Rev Jones, Mary, Wynne and Jack at Wolvesnewton

I know very little of Wynne's early life. I know only that when the family returned to the UK, they settled in Wales where John Jones took up the position of Vicar at Wolvesnewton Church near Chepstow and the family lived at the Vicarage. This would have been Wynne's childhood home. It was where his parents still lived when he went to war.

Wynne was educated at Honiton School in Devon, most probably on some kind of eclesiastical scholarship. In 1913 he went to Canada, where his mother Mary had a sister and possibly where his brother John (Jack) had gone. Wynne began his training in law and was articled as a clerk for five years.

I b. Military Service and Life 1914-1917

At the outbreak of war, Wynne was 18 years of age. He was living in Saskatchewan, Canada where he was articled as a Clerk to Rufus Redmond Earle, a Barrister of the Supreme Court of Saskatchewan with the firm of Barristers, Earl & Keith.

He had begun his clerkship on 23 May 1913 for a period of five years. So clearly Wynne was looking forward to a legal career, quite possibly in Canada. I'm not certain why he had chosen to read law in Canada, I assume having a maternal aunt and possibly his older brother Jack there was at least in part the reason.

Wynne's Canadian Expeditionary Force cap badge

However, at the outbreak of war on 5th August 1914, in order to secure his passage home, Wynne joined the Canadian Infantry and, presumably following basic training of some kind, set out for Britain with the Canadian Expeditionary Force to serve his country.

Like so many of his generation, Wynne seems not to have hesitated a moment in putting to one side his emergent career to serve his country, even though all the talk at the time was of the war being over by Christmas. He might well have been able to avoid serving simply by being in Canada, but I imagine the thought never entered his head.

So it was, that as a serving Canadian Infantry Soldier, Wynne arrived back in the UK and on 5th December 1915 and was commissioned to serve in France with the 9th Battalion Royal Welch Fusiliers as a Temporary Second Lieutenant.

Wynne and Hywel

Again I have very few details regarding Wynne's service in France other than those surrounding his actions leading to his injury and the awarding of his Military Cross. I do know, from his brother Hywel's letters home, that Wynne was in France once again in early 1917 because Hywel comments on what a shame it is that they did not manage to meet up.

Hywel could not possibly have understood as he wrote those words just how much of a tragedy it would prove to be. Just days later he was killed in an utterly pointless incident on the Somme. Wynne of course lived on but all too briefly. The two brothers would never see each other again in this world.

I am all too well aware that these were just two deaths amongst thousands. Our family archive has allowed me to 'bring them to life' somewhat 100 years on, which clearly will not have been the case for many. I hope this book helps us all to remember, honour and reflect upon the incredible loss their generation endured. They called this The Great War – the war to end all wars, and yet within a generation it was to become known as World War 1.

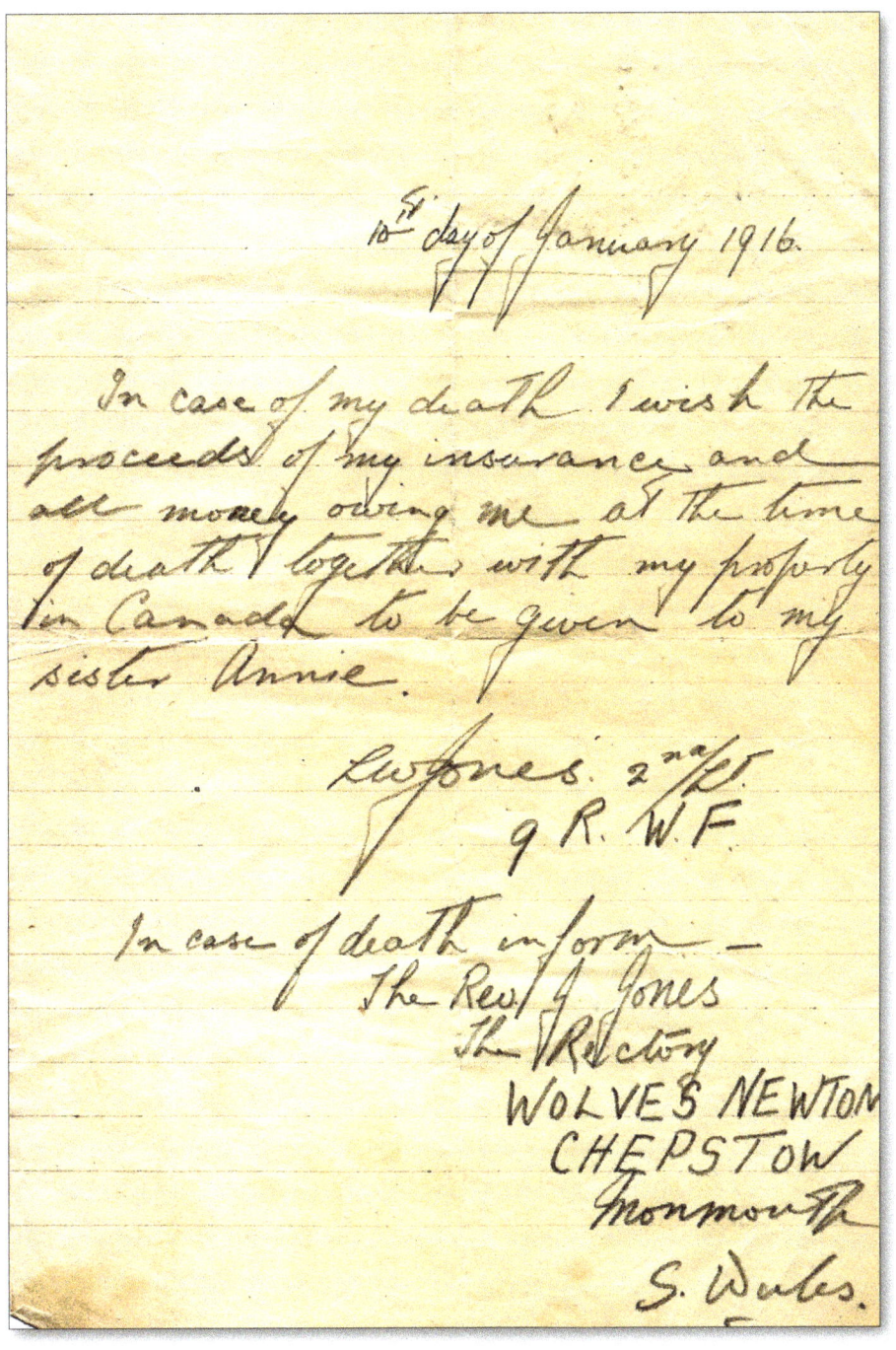

Wynne's hand (pencil) written will - 1916

A particularly interesting and poignant document I have is Wynne's handwritten last will and testament dated 10th January 1916.

I think most soldiers were encouraged to write such documents, but the rough and ready nature of it feels visceral. It is written in pencil and refers to property he apparently had in Canada of which I have no knowledge.

Wynne was to be wounded while on patrol in the Ferme du Bois sector of the Western Front on the 2nd April 1916. He was subsequently awarded the Military Cross with a General Citation reflecting good and brave work over a period of time, but no specific, individual action is recorded.

I do know that he took a bullet to the back of his neck at this time and efforts to surgically remove it via his mouth proved unsuccessful. As a result, he suffered what were referred to by the family as 'episodes' which I take now to have been epilepsy.

In spite of these injuries and the fact that they would probably have enabled Wynne to end his service there, he re-joined his battalion in December 1916. He was then promoted to the rank of Temporary Lieutenant on 1st July 1917 and went on to serve in various attachments including East Africa where, of course, he wrote the diary that started this whole project.

Wynne and Gwladys on their wedding day

Between his service on the Western Front and his departure for East Africa, Wynne married my grandmother, Gwladys Nicholas.

I have no idea when, where or how they met, maybe Gwladys was involved with Red Cross work while Wynne was recovering, I know that she served in this way later on. Or maybe Wynne met Gwladys' father, Alfred through Freemasonry and was introduced to the family in this way, I will never know.

What I do know is that on 3rd October 1917 they were married.

There are many family photos of the occasion taken in the gardens of The Grange in Maesteg, where the Nicholas family lived.

The slips to (no doubt) go in with gifts of cake, as with so many communications of the time, were tiny. The little envelope is barely four inches long. Paper was not wasted as it is today - we could learn a lot!

It's also clear from these slips that the family are already calling themselves "Wynne-Jones" when in reality they are plain Joneses.

The family story was always that Wynne combined his middle and surnames when he began as a barrister because Jones was too common a name to stand out on the Welsh Circuit.

The wedding cake gift cards

However, this invitation would seem to say otherwise. I shall never know the truth – I'm not even sure it was ever official.

Given what we know from his diary, namely that by new year 1918 he was in Port Elizabeth, South Africa, it is clear that Wynne must have embarked for his African tour of duty within a couple of weeks of the marriage.

I always reflect that he must surely have been able to absent himself from further service with his honour intact. He had been significantly wounded in action, still had shrapnel in his neck/skull and was suffering 'episodes' as a result. I can only assume he actively chose not to end his service here.

Wynne seems to have enjoyed soldiering, and indeed to have been rather good at it. Perhaps there was also the matter of it being extremely hard to adjust to civilian life following active service, but whatever his reason for returning to active service in 1917 it was not to be the last time he made this choice. In 1919, having survived the Western Front and East Africa Wynne went on to volunteer for service in Russia fighting the Bolsheviks.

Of course once the war was fully over, he had no option but to re-engage with his civilian life, but even then, he chose to establish a Territorial Army Unit in Maesteg. The 7th (Cyclist) Battalion the Welch Regiment was established in 1920 under the command of Captain Llewellyn Wynne Jones. Ironically, after all the active service Wynne had seen, it was to be during service commanding this TA unit that he would meet his end.

I c. Medal Group

Wynne's medals, which are held in the Regimental Museum

Military Cross Bar
The Military Cross (MC) is the third-level military decoration awarded to officers and (since 1993) other ranks of the British Armed Forces, and used to be awarded to officers of other Commonwealth countries. It is granted in recognition of "an act or acts of exemplary gallantry during active operations against the enemy on land to all members, of any rank in Our Armed Forces".

1914 -15 Star
The 1914–15 Star was instituted in December 1918 and was awarded to officers and men of British and Imperial forces who served against the Central European Powers in any theatre of the Great War between 5 August 1914 and 31 December 1915. The period of eligibility was prior to the Military Service Act 1916, which introduced conscription in Britain.

British War Medal (BWM)
The British War Medal was instituted on 26 July 1919 for award to those who had rendered service between 5 August 1914, the day following the British declaration of war against the German Empire, and the armistice of 11 November 1918, both dates inclusive.

Victory Medal (VM)
The Victory Medal (also called the Inter-Allied Victory Medal) is a United Kingdom and British Empire First World War campaign medal. It was issued to all who received the 1914 Star or the 1914–15 Star, and to most who were awarded the British War Medal - it was not awarded singly. These three medals were sometimes irreverently referred to as Pip, Squeak and Wilfred.

Africa General Service (AGS)
The Africa General Service Medal, established in 1902, was a campaign medal of the United Kingdom. It was awarded for minor campaigns that took place in tropical Africa between 1900 and 1956, with a total of forty five clasps issued. The medal is never seen without a clasp and some are very rare. Most medals were granted to British led local forces, including the King's African Rifles and the West African Frontier Force. The only campaigns where European troops were present in any numbers were the various Somaliland campaigns, (including to the Royal Navy), and in Kenya.

Bar E. Africa 1918
This bar was awarded to local forces employed in operations against the Turkana and other tribes near the South Sudan border.

I d. Diary and Photo Albums

The original diary was given to Wynne by Gwladys as he departed for South Africa just weeks after their wedding on 3rd October 1917.

He was already a keen amateur photographer and took his photographic equipment with him.

Africa would have been a very exotic destination in 1918 not to say somewhat daugnting, but clearly as a young officer Wynne hoped in his photographs to capture something of the continent and his activities there.

After Wynne's untimely death, Gwladys kept the diary and photograph albums. I'm sure she would also have kept the many letters Wynne wrote to her from Africa but tragically they have not survived. Perhaps Grandma felt them too personal to be shared.

In 1982, some five years after my grandmother's death, my father gave me the diary and albums. This was, of course, before home computing and so I set about transcribing the spidery writing by hand into a spare desk diary.

Fascinating as it is to our family, I have never been sure what to do with this archive until now, but I am delighted to be part of ensuring his experiences and his memory live on for future generations to read about.

I e. 1917 Photos from Albums

There are a few photos in Wynne's albums which are obviously part of this campaign but were clearly taken before the diary begins on 1st January 1918. I include them here for completeness.

Lion's Head Cape Town

Sands at Muizenberg

Surf at Muizenberg

The boat I came out on

This photograph in particular is in very poor condition but it seems to me quite an important part of the story given the title grandfather gave it.

I love this shot of a group of Wynne's comrades. They are not mentioned in the diary, but they do look as though they are all starting out together.

Gilbert, Pat, Simpson, Hill, MacLean

This is a lovely picture of Wynne with a fellow officer called MacLean. I love the near essay he wrote on the back of it teasing at Rhodes' photographic skills.

To me these images just look like "calm before the storm" pictures – relaxing together.

MacLean & self outside my hut, old Rhodes took it so it is not in the center

These are photos from Wynne's album plainly taken at sea. He labelled none of them, so there is no way to know when they were taken.

I had hoped at least one of these were images was of a German ship called the Konigsberg[2] - which was famously scuttled in 1915 when she retreated to the Rufigi delta to repair her engines following damage sustained in the Battle Zanzibar.

Sadly I think they are not (though I'm not completely certain, as it would have been considerably plundered over a four year period), but the pictures certainly illustrate that sea travel in 1919 was not without its dangers.

I think Wynne would have taken these three pictures to show the new "dazzle"[3] camouflage employed on ships in 1914-18. He hasn't labelled any of them so I've no idea what or where they are, but I do know they may well have been in very bright colours. The aim was to make it more difficult for enemy submarines to assess the size, shape, course and range of ships.

PART II

1918 Diary

East Africa Campaign

II a. January – March 1918

Tuesday 1 January 1918

When I was called this morning, we were in East London having taken about 12 hours to come from Port Elizabeth, having the mine nippers out takes off about 1 mile per hour.
A great number have sore heads this morning after last night and I am not at all surprised. No shore leave was granted today after the exhibition yesterday, I suppose it was the only thing to do but it was very hard luck on the innocent.
Looking through field glasses, East London seemed a very filthy place indeed, but it is unfortunate it is not a better port so that the mail boats could go alongside instead of having all the trouble of getting your cargo onto
lighters and off again.
It started to rain this afternoon and has been raining ever since.
Left East London at seven.

Port Elizabeth from the Sea

And so Wynne, your journey begins. You are on board a ship arriving at East London, having come from Port Elizabeth. You must have taken this photo as you left.

I've no idea how long your journey has been so far. It can't have been less than four to six weeks I think, so you will have left shortly after your marriage to Gwladys. Does that feel an age ago already I wonder.

Reading this diary today and particularly this first entry, I feel nervous for you not knowing what dangers and privations you will face.

Wednesday 2 January 1918

We kept well in sight of land most of the day but did not arrive in Durban till 8.30 and as it was late, we anchored outside.
There is very rapid current running north to south of about five miles per hour which, helped by nasty wind was the cause of our delay, in peace time it is only a fourteen hour trip from East London to Durban.
I wrote a letter to Gwladys today hoping that a mail will be leaving Durban very shortly.
They had a farewell concert to-night but I'm afraid that the singing was not of the best although some were really quite good.
It has been quite warm today and one feels that the tropical regions are near.
Durban looking very pretty at night all lighted up with no fear of air raids.

Thursday 3 January 1918

We had to be up awfully early this morning, I actually had a bath by 6.30, the earliest I have ever had since I left England.
Eleven of us were split from the draft and had to report at the next camp. The remainder were supposed to go aboard the Coronia[4] but I am told that the NCOs refused to go, the first time I have known of 250 NCOs refusing to obey an order and, in my opinion, they were very silly to give in to them; their complaint was that the boat was lousy, as if they had never been lousy before. I am extremely grieved over the whole affair and I am very glad that I was not left in charge.
The rest camp seems a very nice place and the messing is excellent.
I had tea in Durban and took a spool of films to be developed.
It rained quite heavily (in) the evening and I understand that they have had rather severe floods in the district recently and that they have never known such bad weather for this time of the year.

The Coronia

I found this photo of the 'lousy' Coronia Wynne. I imagine conditions must have been pretty dire, because as you say, the men would have been lousy often enough before they embarked.

Friday 4 January 1918

Got up about eight and heard that all the officers and men were coming into camp off The Caronia which was to be disinfected before proceeding any further.
I went down town this morning to see the paymaster but found him out so left a requisition.
I got my negatives and did some printing before and after lunch and am very pleased with the results. They are rather dark, but the detail is clear.
Saw the Paymaster again this afternoon when he sanctioned an advance of £5 only which we are to call for tomorrow morning. I think it a perfect disgrace that they have not made adequate arrangements for our pay while en route. The weather is simply terrible; it is quite cold and raining very hard indeed.

The Esplanade in Durban c. 1915

I wonder if this is a view you would remember Wynne. The esplanade at Durban. I'm hoping to add photos relating to some of the places you talk about to help us all 'see' a little of your journey.

I am so glad that you are able to get the photographic equipment you needed because you have left us all a wonderful record of your time in Africa.

You are right about the photographic detail Wynne; this photo of Rhodes is simply wonderful. I've no idea if you knew each other before Africa, but, as we shall see further on in this diary, he is clearly an important friend and comrade who was with you right from the start.

Rhodes after getting our kit into hut at Durban

Saturday 5 January 1918

*Went to the Paymaster this morning and actually got £5 out of him,
some were not quite so fortunate.
I purchased some photographic materials this morning and occupied most of the afternoon by
printing some to send to Gwladys.
I went for a walk after dinner as there is really nothing to do in camp
and it is too crowded for comfort.
It was frightfully cold last night and this morning it was awfully showery, but it turned out a
beautiful morning.
We have a church parade tomorrow by order of His Majesty the King.
A special international service.
The news about the food question at home appears to be gloomy.*

It must have been frustrating not being able to get money easily, though as you moved away from towns and into the bush that can only have got worse.

I have wondered how you managed to do so much photography Wynne, but obviously you got in supplies when you could.

Did you post the photographs home or were they too precious to risk in the post I wonder. If you did, it must have been wonderful for Gwladys and the family to receive them. Today's technology means that your family receive pictures of where you are all the time, so it can be hard for us to imagine just how much of a thrill receiving such images would have been in 1918.

This entry in the back of your diary shows that you began to record the supplies you bought, but I don't think you kept it up as there is only this one entry. No doubt, life became more and more busy.

THE ROAD OF DONKEY BONES : A 1918 DIARY FROM BRITAIN'S WW1 EAST AFRICA CAMPAIGN

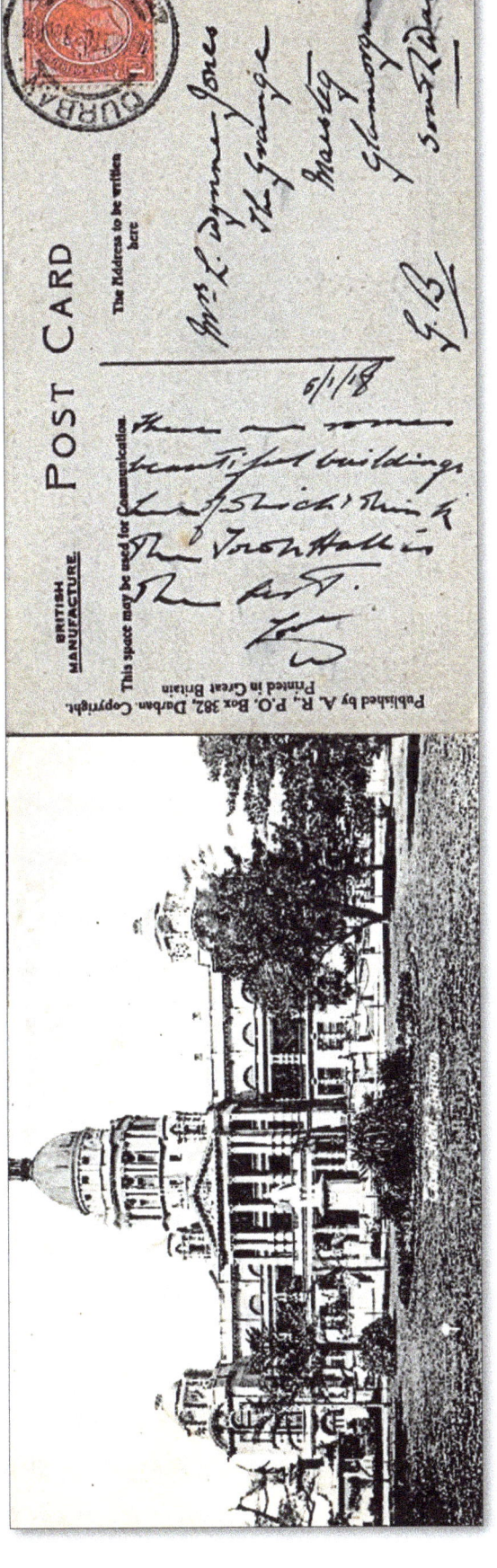

Sunday 6 January 1918

Had a special service this morning in the church hall Durban, which is a magnificent building, about 3000 troops were present, and it was quite a good service. Went on the beach in the early part of the afternoon had tea and then went to Lungin where they have recently had terrible floods, two bridges have been washed clear away and several natives losing their lives and the sugar crops were ruined.
I did some developing after supper. The fourteens are going to be left here still what for I don't know but I don't expect to be here long. It was quite a nice day although it rained a little in the morning.

This is the only item of mail I have from all the letters that you sent to grandma and I have included it here Wynne because it is from Durban and is dated 6 January 2018.

To me, it is such a lovely personal item, it gives me goose bumps. Though I so wish all the other letters that you two wrote to each other had survived. I know grandma would have kept them, but I guess she disposed of them in a timely manner too, preferring to keep them private between you two.

The postcard reads:

There are some beautiful buildings here
of which I think The Town Hall is the best.
Love
W

Monday 7 January 1918

*Went down to the beach in the morning to see the swimming. I think I shall go down tomorrow.
I wrote to Gwladys a little this afternoon and then had a rest.
After tea I went with Rhodes and Pat to the zoo but as we arrived late, we only had a quarter
of an hour in which to see the sights. It is a very interesting little zoo and
we intend to pay it another visit before we leave.
After dinner I went with Rhodes to a variety show at The Criterion, it was one of the worst
performances I have ever seen. I think that it was even worse than the show I saw at Cape Town.
It has been a lovely day some have been complaining of the heat, but I thought it was just nice.*

The Criterion Theatre, Durban

It is so good to read about all the sights you are seeing and the ways in which you keep yourselves entertained. You would have been enjoying life while you could Wynne, although The Criterion show sounds to have left a lot to be desired, you know this is the calm before the storm, so enjoy what you can.

Surely you walked down the esplanade when you went to see the swimming and I think the theatre is at the end of that. You would be truly amazed at the internet 100 years on!

I found this photograph of The Criterion which I hope would be familiar to you, though no doubt in 1918 it would have been surrounded by soldiers.

I do hope you might recognise it though because being able to visualise all the places you visited really helps me to bring your diary to life.

Tuesday 8 January 1918

*Went down for a swim this morning and enjoyed it very much, got slightly sun burnt.
Went on circular route this afternoon and saw Musgrave Road which passes through the residential part of Durban, we broke the journey at the zoo and had a better look around than we had yesterday.
It started to rain before dinner which spoilt a really glorious day it was 80° in the shade.
I wrote to Gwladys after dinner, I must finish the letter off as the mail for England is leaving very shortly.*

I wonder as I read this, if you were thinking of living abroad with Gwladys when all of this was over Wynne. How different my life would have been if you had – though actually I might never have existed! All life truly is a matter of chance.

Musgrave Road was a nice quiet residential area in your time but I'm sure today it would be unrecognisable to you, probably subsumed into the city centre.

I am glad you were able to get a better look at the zoo today. I wonder if anyone went off on safari back then, it seems rather odd to go to a zoo in a country where all that wildlife is just out there on your doorstep.

Wednesday 9 January 1918

*Had my usual swim, but it was very cold out of the water.
It has rained practically the whole day.
Went to the Town Hall after dinner to see the picture "Fall of a Nation"[5]. It was not at all bad.
I suspect we will leave here shortly, and I would not be surprised if we go after Von Lettow[6] who appears to be giving the Portuguese a very warm time taking their armies and equipping his own nations.
I am afraid the Portuguese are short of guts.
Finished letter to Gwladys.*

The Town Hall in Durban certainly is a very impressive building Wynne, but I wonder why it is being used as a cinema. Perhaps it is a somewhat political showing, this film was essentially a piece of American propaganda I think and a rallying cry to that nation.

But you enjoyed it, so that has to be a good thing. Though I get the sense it has also meant your thoughts are now turning more to the job in hand and the enemy you are yet to face.

As someone who had already served on the Western Front, it must have been quite interesting to see how that was portrayed. I wonder what your impressions were.

I know that the Portuguese actions in East Africa were not well thought of.

Thursday 10 January 1918

A very wet day and rather cold. I went around the Museum and Art Gallery in the morning. Read some Scotch Law in the afternoon we went into town for tea and then went to see the Botanical Gardens which is in a rather untidy condition.
Went for a walk in the evening on to the front as it had cleared up.

The Botanical Gardens sounds to be suffering somewhat. Perhaps the war means there is less effort being put into their upkeep and less available labour to do the work. Nevertheless, it must have been a relaxing place for a stroll.

Friday 11 January 1918

A swim in the morning as it was really a lovely day. Finished off letters as the English mails closed at four. Went downtown to port around 3.30 then had tea and a walk along the front. Went with Rhodes in the evening to see "The Country that God Forgot", it was a very disappointing picture indeed.
Was Orderly Officer today.

Swimming baths, Durban

I love this picture from your album Wynne. It looks so normal, hard to believe you are at war and on your way into battle. Obviously, you went here, but quite how often you swam in the sea and how often you used the baths I've no idea.

Saturday 12 January 1918

Swim in the morning. The water was lovely and warm. Turned out a very (wet) afternoon.
I luckily managed to do some printing before it came on.
Had tea downtown then went to The Club to read the papers.
After dinner I went back to The Club to watch billiards.
I don't think we shall be here much longer.

The Club, Durban

It must have been dreadful just waiting to go off to fight. You have clearly made the most of Durban's distractions Wynne, but at the end of the day the tedium and the sense of the uncertainty must have made it difficult for you to truly relax and enjoy yourselves. There is a real sense of foreboding mixed with boredom in your entry here.

I'm not sure if this is the place you refer to as The Club. It does look incredibly posh though and utterly British - so I really hope it is and that it felt like some real home comfort for you all. Overall, I think you should all enjoy as many luxuries as you can while you can.

Sunday 13 January 1918

Went for a swim in the morning but did not enjoy it as the water was more like soup and the crowds were unbearable so did not stay in for long.
It was quite warm in the afternoon so stayed in the hut during the greater part of the time till tea.
Had tea in The Club and then went out to Umbilo getting back in time for dinner.
Went down to the front after dinner till about ten o'clock.

Conditions all round are sounding a little rough today, or maybe it's just that time is beginning to drag and there is a sense of needing to get on with things.

From this picture in your album, I can see that your camp doesn't look like the most glamourous of places. So spending most of the afternoon in your hut due to the heat must have been simply dismal.

No wonder you felt the need to get out and about. Umbilo, where you went after tea is today a central suburb of Durban.

Back in 1918 it was considered a beauty spot complete with a picnic area, waterfall and about 80 mysterious burial mounds. I wonder if you saw all of that Wynne.

Or maybe you were more interested in the ruins of Durban's first waterworks and dam, which were also in Umbilo.

Either way, I hope it was a nice place to relax for a while.

Looking down our camp at residential quarter, Durban

Monday 14 January 1918

Got pay from the Paymaster for £5.
Had swim as usual, it was much nicer than yesterday as the
beach was washed out last night and naturally it was much cleaner.
Went to Overport in the afternoon but found that it was impossible
to obtain tea so returned to town about four.
Went to the Criterion after dinner, the show as a whole was rotten
but there was one girl who sang excellently.
It was nearly 82° in the shade to-day.

Grey Street Mosque, Overport, Durban

This so made me laugh Wynne. How very British of you – no tea available in Overport meant you had to get out of there! Well fair play, a man should have his comforts.

As with Umbilo, Overport is today a suburb of Durban but it always had a significant Indian population, many of whom had arrived to help establish the colonies. Certainly, the Grey Street Mosque would have been there in your day, so I'm hoping this picture is a fair representation of what you saw before you fled for tea.

Tuesday 15 January 1918

Swam in the morning, printed some photos in the afternoon and then went to The Congella Hotel had tea and dinner there after which we played billiards returning to camp around 9.30. It has been quite warm today.

I have chosen these two pictures from your campaign albums Wynne because I love the contrast. The first shows you in near full uniform and second much more relaxed, both outside your hut. I think they were taken at the Durban camp, though you didn't label either.

Whilst I'm sure conditions were less than glamorous; I think this was to be the last you saw of anything as substantial as a wooden hut for a very long time.

Wednesday 16 January 1918

*Went for a swim in the morning. Played tennis this afternoon, the first time since war and I am afraid I was rather out of practice.
I have to play in a match to-morrow, I hope I will do better than I did today.
The weather broke in the evening and it turned out quite nasty and wet.
Developed a film after dinner and did some colour printing.*

Tennis is a new distraction which sounds great Wynne. I have no idea where your colour prints went, I have never seen any, which really is a great shame.

Thursday 17 January 1918

We left camp at 10.30 to play tennis, we started playing at 11. We won by two games my partner was Patterson and we did much better than we did yesterday. The first set lost by 6:4 the second we won 7:2 and the third we lost by 6:3 so on the whole we did not do so badly, and I played much better than I played yesterday.
I attended a lodge this evening in Inanda, Stamford Hill. Got home around 11.30.

I think this picture from your album shows Rhodes on the right (and possibly Patterson) in their tennis whites although you didn't label it, so I can't be sure. They could equally be cricket whites of course. Still, I'm glad that your tennis has improved.

I've often wondered when you became a Free Mason. I know Gwladys' father Alfred Nicholas was, so maybe he introduced you to the lodge, or maybe you were already a Mason and that's how you met the Nicholas' family and Gwladys. I'll never know, I guess.

I did look up Inanda Lodge[7] though and it was established in 1869 in the Durban area. It had over 1000 members.

Friday 18 January 1918

Went out with Rhodes and Patterson to play tennis this morning but I was much too stiff to move. I printed photos most of the afternoon till I went downtown for tea.
Went to The Empire after dinner, it was not too bad. Rained slightly this evening.
Got orders to embark on Monday 21st.

Oh dear Wynne – stiff from yesterday's tennis! I guess you will need to get fit for what is to come. Anyway, I'm glad you enjoyed The Empire, particularly as you now know you have just three more days in Durban.

The Empire, Durban

Saturday 19 January 1918

Went downtown to get some photos back from the chemist.
Did some printing up till lunch.
Went out for tennis in the afternoon but did not finish one set as it simply poured down.
Went out to The Wartsi for the evening and had quite an enjoyable time arriving in camp about 11.30. It rained the whole time from 3pm.

Sunday 20 January 1918

Wrote some letters in the morning and the early part of the afternoon.
Went to The Club for tea and hurried back to camp to finish my letters, I also did some packing in case we had to go on forward to go board tomorrow.
Went with Pat to spend the evening with the Walls had quite an enjoyable evening returning to camp about eleven. Had very heavy showers this evening.

Wynne's contact details

There is a real sense of tension reading between the lines here Wynne. Tomorrow you embark on a journey of huge uncertainty. You don't really know what you will face or even if you will survive, frankly it's hard for me to even imagine.

I found this envelope amongst Gwladys's things. It contains your Africa contact details written in your own hand I think and was clearly a precious memory to her.

Monday 21 January 1918

Had to stand by this morning till eleven when we got orders that we were not embarking till tomorrow. Five minutes after orders came for us to be on board by three so we had a great rush getting our things packed.
Got on board about 2.30 and did not get off again till six when we had a rush to get dinner at The Royal and then go to The Criterion, it was not a bad show.
We got back to the boat, which is called The Gaika, about eleven.

Oh Wynne, what a chaotic embarkation day for you all, I don't know whether to think it was good in the end or not.

I do think it was good that you managed to get off for some dinner though, particularly as it was at The Royal which is clearly a very lovely place.

The Royal, Durban

You must all have savoured its wonderfully luxurious surroundings. Though it would surely have seemed almost surreal given what was ahead. Strange too for the staff who would have served way too many young men enjoying their last comforts there. They probably had a far better idea about what was ahead for you all.

Tuesday 22 January 1918

When I got up this morning the boat was well out of port.
I understand she started off at about five.
There is a very nasty ground swell in these parts which makes the old tub roll very badly indeed.
This boat is a quite small one and is about 25 years old. I think she would be quite comfortable in peace time and if one was not in too great a hurry, her maximum is
only 11 per hour.
We are rather overcrowded for warm climes.
Old Pat was sick this evening.

The Gaika

From what you say about overcrowding Wynne, I'm sure that this 1914 image of The Gaika[8] loaded with troops in East Africa is pretty accurate. The old tub rolling heavily must have been awful. I can only begin to imagine how hideous conditions on board would have been.

Wednesday 23 January 1918

I woke up this morning feeling unfit this morning, but I tried to eat some breakfast but only got as far as the porridge when I had to leave in a hurry, but it was the only meal I did miss.
I lay down practically the whole day except when I took my meals.

Thursday 24 January 1918

*A very rough night had great difficulty in remaining on my couch bed on account of the roll.
It rained the greater part of the day.
Read all day. It is very warm in the cabin this evening.*

Friday 25 January 1918

As calm as a duck pond but getting rather warm. Read and wrote letters the whole day.

Saturday 26 January 1918

*Absolutely nothing fresh today. Still
keeps fine and keeping warm. Hope to be in port by Tuesday morning.*

Sunday 27 January 1918

Wrote letters most of the morning and lolled around. Did not seem quite so warm, still awfully calm.

Monday 28 January 1918

*Continued the letters in the morning finishing them off after dinner.
Got my kit ready in case we go ashore tomorrow.
Got rather rough during the evening and it is none too smooth
at the present moment.*

For those of you (like me) whose geographical knowledge of East Africa is poor, this map shows how far it is from Durban to Dar es Salaam. Nearly half the length of Africa. So, it is a 7-day trip and in 1918 was not without risk. Many ships were attacked in these waters.

N.B. This is a modern map, so the country names and borders will not be accurate to 1918.

Tuesday 29 January 1918

*Arrived in sight of Dar es Salaam about 8.30 and my first impression
was not good as it all seemed very low lying making it unhealthy.
The native troops were taken off in lighters about eleven, but the boat did not actually go into
the harbour till 5pm. It is really a splendid harbour and the Germans must have
spent a great deal of money on it.
We understood we were to land this evening, so we had everything packed when the order was
suddenly cancelled, so had to get out a few things for the night.*

Dar es Salaam Harbour

I must say Wynne, I'm glad that you have arrived safely. Naval warfare was common, and though you say nothing about it, your seven days at sea were very dangerous. All of the colonial powers had naval squadrons stationed in the Indian or Pacific Oceans and troop ships were certainly a target.

It must also be a relief to be off the dear old Gaika though. I imagine the cramped conditions, rough seas and heat must have resulted in some pretty unsanitary conditions.

I'm not sure if this is the "splendid harbour" you describe. I know that the German East Africa Company constructed one in the late 1800s under colonial rule, but this is all I could find.

Wednesday 30 January 1918

Our luggage went to land in a tug, but I went along with Rhodes in a rowing boat, landed on the first occupied territory I had been on since the war and found the Germans were still running their trades on arrival and that there are plenty of German women still around, but they are not allowed down to the front.
I had lunch in the mess of the detail camp which is situated in a very sandy spot in the centre of coconut palms and everything is simply covered with sand.
How one undresses at night without getting sand all over one beats me.
I share a tent with Rhodes which is really only meant for one, but we extended it by propping up the sides.

Camp I stayed in for eight days, my tent is the second in the first row from the left of small tents

Dar es Salaam is a long way further north Wynne, nearer the equator and so maybe a lot hotter. That will also mean more dust and sand of course. The camp conditions do sound horrible, you must all have been very uncomfortable.

Although it must be a bit more of a crush, perhaps it is quite nice to be sharing a tent with Rhodes.

This picture from your album I think shows the camp you describe here. It looks wonderfully ordered but not terribly comfortable. Lovely to have the tent you shared with Rhodes highlighted – I do wish you had given this much detail on the back of all your photos.

Thursday 31 January 1918

We both obtained a boy last night, but it is absolutely necessary to be able to talk Swahili else you never get anything done, but ours will pick it up very quickly when he knows it is the only way he can get anything, the one I have seems quite clean and works fairly well but I don't know whether to take him up to Nairobi or not or risk getting a good one there.
I went down the town in the morning to do a little shopping.
I went to the YMCA for a concert and found it was really very good. I did not arrive back in camp till 11.00 having to get into bed in the dark as I could not find my matches.
Had a swim in the sea this evening.

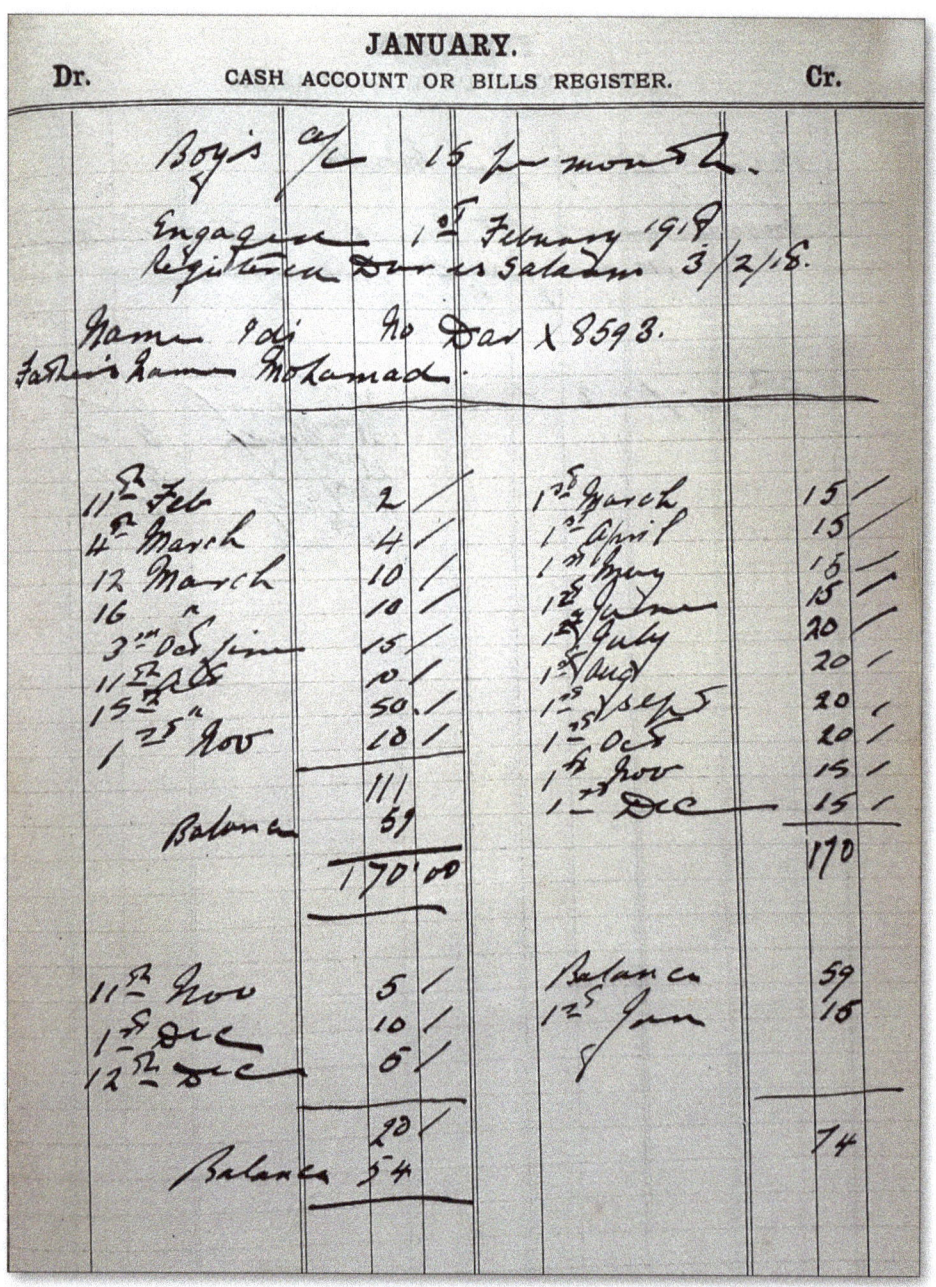

Now Wynne, you can't even imagine how awful it sounds in 2018 to say you 'obtained a boy' but I'm sure it would have been the norm. I assume he is a sort of house boy/servant.

I found this page in the back of your diary where you have documented the young fellow. His name is Idi and his father is Mohamed and you appear to have agreed to pay him 15 (somethings) a month.

I've no idea how you would have paid or if this was a fair amount, perhaps it was organised through the military. There is reference to his being registered with the number 8593, so I guess it is all official.

I've no idea what little Idi was expected to do, but I do hope that he did okay with his new master and that he wasn't too young for whatever lay ahead. I wonder too how willing he was. I know that a great many porters had precious little say about their involvement. Either way, I hope you were kind to him, he is just a child.

Friday 1 February 1918

Went downtown to draw £5 which was given me in single rubber bits, and they were some weight. Wrote letters in the afternoon. Went to the YMCA concert again after dinner.

I have no idea what 'single rubber bits' refers to, but in trying to research it I did find an excellent piece by John E. Sandrock[9] on the internet which provides a really interesting overview of the problems with currency in WW1 in East Africa. Again, you would be amazed at the internet Wynne.

The piece made me realise that what I had taken for some kind of chit held in the pages of your diary was in fact something called a Bush Note and, something you may not have been aware about, a particularly interesting one.

The Germans had constant problems with Deutsch Osta Afrikanische Bank (DOAB) notes, literally running out which made it difficult to pay porters and buy supplies. They struggled to access the equipment and paper needed to print the notes.

This is what John E Sandrock had to say about it and it's of particular relevance to your note:

"This problem, like all others, was overcome by ingenuity. The Germans had come across a farm while crossing the Rufiji valley where they found a child's plaything with which to solve the problem. This was a toy printing press, complete with movable rubber type used for making hand stamps. Not too pretty, but very functional! It was quickly pressed into service to make more notes."

From the description Sandrock gives, which details the signatures and stamps used, it is clear that your note is one of those manufactured in the Rufiji Valley using a child's printing press.

Saturday 2 February 1918

*Was on duty at 7 at the petrol dump which meant me getting up at 5 and I am afraid I did not have much breakfast only a slice of bread and jam and a cup of tea.
It rained off and on this early morning, so I got wet several times and had to allow it to dry on me with the result that my knees and arms were badly burnt and they are very painful this morning.
Did not get back to camp till 2 when I had what lunch I could get and then printed photos.
Got to bed early for a change after writing to Gwladys.*

What a very miserable day Wynne. Hot, wet, long and dreary. War is rarely glorious and exciting is it, just hard work, massive discomfort and a lot of pain.

Sunday 3 February 1918

*My arms were rather badly blistered this morning and I am afraid they will give me trouble.
Fixed some photos to send home, they are really quite good.
Slept most of the afternoon to see if I could cure my arms but without any luck as they are giving me awful pain this evening.
Went for a walk after dinner.*

Poor Wynne, your arms sound really sore. Amongst the many potentially health protecting things the British army appear not to have provided in 1918 is, of course, sunscreen. To be fair, it really wasn't widely available until WW2.

Monday 4 February 1918

*Went downtown in the morning and then went outside the harbour for a sail and arranged for this boat to come for us in the afternoon but it failed to turn up worse luck.
I had the usual swim after tea.
My arms are sore tonight, so I have bandaged them up to try and keep them clean.
Finished letter to Gwladys.*

I'm not sure what type of sailing boat trip you had planned, but dhows were in common use. To be honest though Wynne, with your sunburnt arms, I think the 'no show' may have been for the best.

Tuesday 5 February 1918

I went down for a swim before breakfast as well as after tea.
My arms are a little better, but the right is still very raw, and I shall have to keep it covered.
Was on a Court of Enquiry this morning but it only lasted about half an hour.
The Mess here is simply awful and I have not had a meal since I have been here.

Looker, Simpson, McLean, Smith

Good to hear that your arms are improving. I don't know what medical help was available in camp, but I am using this entry to include your lovely picture of nurses and doctors.

Though I'm sure that your colleagues relaxing with the medical team here would have had more to do with pretty nurses than health care Wynne. A bit of female company must have been lovely for you all – and I think for the nurses too.

Wednesday 6 February 1918

Nothing doing at all, am getting more fed up with the camp every day.
We have orders to leave on Friday.

Dar es Salaam just doesn't have the distractions of Durban does it Wynne. That must be frustrating as you wait to go up country. I can sense your restlessness here. Perhaps you are all feeling a bit like it's the calm before the storm now. Not busy enough, not enough distractions but uncertain dangers before you. You must just want to get on with it now.

Thursday 7 February 1918

*Got things ready for tomorrow as the baggage has to be ready by 6.30 which will mean 8.30.
they always order the baggage to be ready hours before necessary.
Went out to the YMCA Cinema this evening, the pictures were not very good.*

All packed up and ready to go now Wynne. I hope the embarkation will prove to be better organised than last time. Next stop Mombasa I believe, and it sounds as though you won't be too sad to leave Dar.

A shame that the pictures weren't so good for your last night in Dar es Salaam but good on the YMCA[10] for providing their support to our men way out in East Africa.

Friday 8 February 1918

*Got up about 5.30 saw that my kit was packed.
I paid 24.70 for messing. I never grudged money quite so much in the whole of my life.
I got on board The Umtata at 11 but did not sail till five. She is a rotten boat, most of us slept on deck but fortunately I had a cabin which saved me unpacking my bed which would have been awkward as my boy was very seasick.
The food was not much good on board, I shall be very glad when I can sit down to eat a square meal.*

I have learnt an awful lot researching around your diary entries Wynne. Although I could find no images of The Umtata, you might be interested in the following background.

The Umtata was a Natal Direct Line ship. The Natal Direct Line was so named because before the war their vessels by-passed the Cape of Good Hope and proceeded direct to Durban - or Port Natal as it was more commonly known then.

Umtata was a name given to at least four of their boats, the one you travelled on was probably the first or second. The company always used Zulu names for their ships and so far as I can ascertain Umtata means Father in Zulu – but I'm no expert.

Poor young Idi is clearly not used to sailing. I hope he feels better soon.

Saturday 9 February 1918

Arrived Mombasa about midday. Had lunch on board and then went to report as Rhodes was not at all well. We decided to stay in The Metropole Hotel.
We had a decent dinner at last after walking around the town and getting our boys to stay by our kits.
Turned in very early as we have to be on the train by 7 tomorrow morning.

I'm so glad that you and Rhodes managed to get a decent night at The Metropole Hotel Wynne, it must be a worry not feeling well when you are both just off to, well heaven knows where, but definitely somewhere fairly remote and harsh.

Those troop ships must have been awful. I know that they were generally extremely overcrowded with soldiers sleeping all over the decks, so one can only imagine what it would have been like when the sea was rough, and the men were seasick.

I found this old post card of The Metropole Hotel from 1910 Wynne. I think it would be a familiar image to you and it certainly looks more comfortable than a troop ship overloaded with seasick soldiers – though frankly almost anything does!

I do hope Rhodes feels better soon.

Sunday 10 February 1918

Had breakfast about six then motored to the station. We departed about 7.30 in a troop train, there were four to a carriage and as there are four bunks, we ought to be quite comfortable.
We passed through some very pretty country at the beginning but after that everything was very bare and dry.
We stopped at every station on the way up which made the journey very tedious. I read most of the time and turned in about eight.

I found this wonderful pre-war poster for the Uganda Railway Wynne, no doubt produced for the burgeoning tourist industry in the early 1900s.

It's probably me, but the line *'step by step through nature's zoo'* really makes me laugh – as though nature involves a zoo!

Of course, it would have been a very exotic trip back then and I imagine there was a part of you that was quite excited. Perhaps you planned to take Gwladys to see all these wonders after the war.

As with everything else, I'm sure that the conversion of these methods of transport to troop (and equipment) carriers definitely removed the luxury edge.

Monday 11 February 1918

Arrived in Nairobi about 12.30 after getting all our kit on to a motor lorry. Rhodes and I went up with it to the Detail camp and then had lunch.
I got four letters this evening, one from Gwladys, one from home, one from Annie and one from Canada; Gwladys' was written on the 29th, three days after I left, it has bucked me up a lot, I am afraid that it will be a matter of luck to whether she gets letters or not.
Went for a walk into Nairobi after tea and it did not strike me as being very great.
As we are 6000 ft up it was frightfully cold this evening.
Paid boy 2 chips.

Nairobi Station

I'm guessing that in 1918 Nairobi was simply full of troops Wynne, and there seem to be a few on the platform here. So I hope these photos of Nairobi station would be familiar.

It must have been lovely to have news from pretty much everyone at home, I can tell how much of a boost that is for you.

I hope they are also getting your letters. It seems quite extraordinary to me that they managed to keep the post going in wartime between Africa and Wales – that must have been quite an operation, but I guess it was a recognition of how vital these links were for moral.

Tuesday 12 February 1918

*Saw paymaster this morning but he was unable to tell us (how) our accounts stood;
I shall be glad when it is settled up as I owe £10.
Saw A.A.G. this afternoon and found that I was posted to the 3/6 K.A.R. rt In
Bagathi (Mbagathi) about eight miles away.
Stayed in camp rest of the day.*

I spent a good while trying to find Bagathi - in the end Wynne I think you left a silent 'M' off when you wrote it down.

Today it has been absorbed into the city of Nairobi but when you were there, I think it was still quite rural being 8 miles away.

K.A.R. Home, Nairobi

I found these photos in your album which must be of the Kings African Rifles camp you refer to.

It's great to be able to see exactly where you were. If only you'd labelled all your photos so well!

You don't say anything about your posting to the 3/6 Kings African Rifles. Are you pleased with that I wonder? Impossible to know, but I guess it is all starting to get very real now.

View from the K.A.R. House

Wednesday 13 February 1918

*Went down to Nairobi to buy a few odds and ends before we go out into the country.
Had lunch at the New Stanley.
Slept most of the afternoon.*

The New Stanley Hotel, Nairobi

Well done Wynne, you are still managing to find places to have a good meal and a bit of comfort before you head out into the bush. Enjoy it while you can.

I always imagine that you are identifying places to stay and things to see with Gwladys when the war is over. Do you write and tell her about them? Do you plan together for the adventures you will have in the future?

I found this post card of the New Stanley which does look rather nice. Again, I can only hope it's a familiar image to you and therefore helps me to see things as you saw them and imagine you there.

Thursday 14 February 1918

Had to get our kits packed by 9.30, we saw them on to a wagon drawn by sixteen oxen and thought they would be there long before us, but they did not arrive till 7 in the evening. We came out in g **** g five of us all told, and it was a very rough ride. We arrived in camp about four, but I am afraid I shall be very fed up with it in no time. We are in tents single ones which of course will not keep out the sand and I am afraid it will be very cold at night.

Oxen - Nairobi

This is a simply magnificent photo Wynne. The oxen must have been quite a sight and I'm glad that you captured it here.

Sometimes I struggle with your writing and I'm afraid I cannot read the name of your transport in line three of today's entry. When I put it on Facebook some suggested gurney was a word in wider use than medicine – but I am really not sure.

Friday 15 February 1918

Did some parades today. It seems very funny to be on parade once more. There are too many South African Officers here for one to like it. I am afraid they will never work well with the Imperial Officers.

It is difficult to understand your take on the world 100 years on Wynne. I know a great deal of rancour remained from the Boer Wars. You clearly aren't as comfortable with colonial as opposed to imperial officers. Maybe you recognise the rancour and think it won't work well?

2018 is very much a post-colonial age. Brits were (and are) very capable of unreasonable arrogance and snobbery, but your life might depend on it all being okay, so I can't judge that.

Much has been written on this subject and I found Andrew Knighton's[11] blog. on General Jan Smuts: "Fighting Snobbery and Germany in East Africa in WW1" very interesting.

THE ROAD OF DONKEY BONES : A 1918 DIARY FROM BRITAIN'S WW1 EAST AFRICA CAMPAIGN

Saturday 16 February 1918

There are no parades on Saturday except 7 to 8 so I wrote and read most of the day after arranging my kit.

Just as you get going there is more hanging around awaiting further orders Wynne. That must be trying. The parades must have helped to relieve the boredom and tension in camp.

Sunday 17 February 1918

I remained in camp all day and wrote.

You took some wonderful photos waiting around in camp Wynne, though it was clearly very dull and frustrating.

These are two of my favourites, you and Rhodes I think with your washing out to dry and it looks as though there are two beds up – are you sharing again? The detail is great.

I particularly love the photo of you (above), it's so wonderfully informal and you look so rakish.

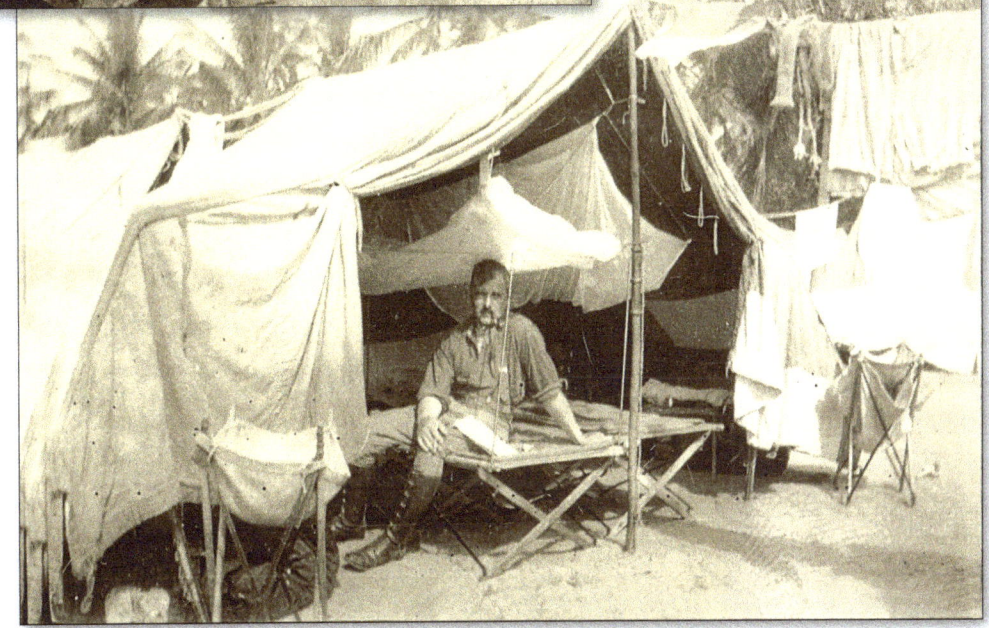

Monday 18 February 1918

Went out for a field day this morning. They are nearly as dangerous as the real thing, we had a hand to hand fight, one native losing a hand and a white Sergeant getting hit through the arm. They are no joke, but I shall be better prepared for the next one, I only had on thin cams which was not much good, but I was lucky to get off with only a bruise on my arm.

I have led such an easy middle-class existence Wynne that it's really hard to imagine this sort of thing. In some ways it must have relieved the boredom, but in others surely quite a malign reminder of things to come.

Tuesday 19 February 1918

We were out all the morning practising field duties, in the afternoon we did squad drill and then Swahili.
I am not feeling at all fit. I had another letter from home.

It is all getting very urgent and busy now isn't it Wynne? Is that a good thing for you? It must be a plus to be busy and engaged.

Obviously, the field duties and drill are testing your fitness levels, so I guess you're feeling a bit stiff. Perhaps learning Swahili is a welcome break today.

Your pictures of field duty are just wonderful, though sadly you didn't label most of them.

Wednesday 20 February 1918

Out again on bush work this morning. Have got my knees well torn now. I slept all the afternoon and I was really unwell. I have a rather nasty boil on the back of my neck which is troubling my head. The dust here is frightful.

Today we have so many excellent modern medicines that would have made your life so much better, not least anti-biotics. It is easy in 2018 to forget that in 1918 a boil on the back of your neck in the middle of Africa very definitely had the potential to kill you.

You took many wonderful pictures of bush training sessions and here is another.

Thursday 21 February 1918

I stayed in all day as I was not feeling at all fit, have to be on the move early tomorrow on a field stunt. Wrote to Gwladys.

I thought the other day when you said you were feeling unfit that you meant physical fitness, because of the field work and drills. It appears now you may have meant that you were not feeling well. Whatever the cause, I hope you feel better soon – you are just at the beginning of things.

I'm adding this lovely picture of my grandma, your Gwladys, here Wynne. She was such a beautiful young woman, no wonder you fell in love with her and wrote to her so often.

Friday 22 February 1918

Went off on a field stunt which I am afraid we rather mucked up there was too much delay before we attacked and then time was so limited that we had to move on the double thus tiring the troops before we got near the enemy. We (were) at it till five.

Goodness Wynne, you must all be physically and mentally exhausted. Though it's obviously good to make your mistakes now and learn your lessons during practice.

This is a lovely picture from your album. I'm sure you could put names to all the faces but sadly for me you didn't write them down. I particularly like the casual, though clearly posed nature of the shot. Is that a Lewis gun? They seem to be very pleased with it anyway.

Saturday 23 February 1918

Took some photos which I developed this evening, the conveniences were not good, but I got some very good negatives.

Sunday 24 February 1918

Printed most of the morning. Did Swahili in the evening.

Monday 25 February 1918

Out on a field day, I have never seen such a muck up in all my life. I thanked my lucky stars more than once that it was not real warfare. No wonder that the war in this country is not over yet, heaven forbid that I have to serve in the field with them. I was dead tired this evening.

Oh Wynne, this must be frightening because you know you will be going to fight together shortly. What are the main issues, is it language and communication? That must be frightening for the native troops as well.

I do know from my research that towards the end of the war (which though you don't know it, is where you are) many ordinary soldiers spoke very highly of the Kings African Rifles as being extremely brave, loyal and effective soldiers who they were proud to have fought with.

Tuesday 26 February 1918

Did bayonet fighting before breakfast and musketing the rest of the day. I have to buck up with my Swahili as there is an exam on Thursday.
I am not feeling at all fit, a nasty boil on the back of my neck is giving me trouble.

Heavens, bayonet fighting before breakfast sounds like quite a wakeup call Wynne. I imagine that must have generated a significant appetite.

I do hope you get some help with the nasty boil soon. It must be very painful.

Wednesday 27 February 1918

Got inoculated today and in Mbagathi Hospital.
Was on the range the early part of the morning and then continued with ordinary parade.
My arm a little painful this evening.

I discovered there is still a hospital in Mbagathi Wynne, it was re-built in the 1950s as today Mbagathi has been subsumed into the city, so you would recognise nothing, I think.

Thursday 1 March 1918

I did not celebrate St David's Day as I usually do, they are nearly all scotch and South Africans. My arm is quite sore to-day. I was on the range again this morning.

Happy St David's Day though Wynne.

Friday 2 March 1918

Only had a parade before breakfast so wrote letters most of the day.

Saturday 3 March 1918

Had walls built of sticks and straw on which I could raise my tent my men did not do it at (all) well. I am afraid I shall have to get it altered.

This is one of the photos from your campaign album and I just wondered if this is the sort of adaptation you are talking about here.

I'm assuming this helped to keep out the sun and the heat, but not sure what the other objectives were. Perhaps it helped to keep the sand down and creepy crawlies at bay – though I'd hate to imagine what might hide in all that straw.

You never really complain about the wildlife Wynne, other than the mosquitoes but I think there must have been spiders, snakes, lizards, massive cockroaches and all manner of horrible parasites. And when you get further into the bush surely lions and other big cats, not to mention hippos.

Perhaps you just ignored it as much as possible, or just got used to sharing your bed with such horrible night-time friends.

Sunday 4 March 1918

*Got up about 4.30 company parade at six, Battalion 6.30.
I am afraid some of the umpire's ideas about soldiering are very vague and want changing. If they only saw a little fighting instead of telling others how to do it, they would do much better.
I am getting more fed up every field day I go on.*

The grave of Hywel Jones in Peronne, France

Although you do not mention it here, I feel sure that this was a very poignant day for you Wynne. It was the first anniversary of your younger brother Hywel's death near Clery sur Somme on the Western Front.

It must have been particularly difficult while dealing with the inadequacies in the training of troops on whom you may soon depend for your own life.

I hope you would be comforted somewhat to know that I visited Hywel's grave in Peronne, to mark the 100th anniversary of his death.

Like so many of your generation, Hywel was too young to make such a sacrifice yet he and thousands like him did their duty and gave their all.

It was marking Hywel's centenary which spurred me on to complete the work on your diary. I hope you would both have been pleased to know you are not forgotten.

Monday 5 March 1918

I am orderly officer and had to supervise kiboko tonight. They don't seem to give it half hard enough.
My eye was rather sore, so the doctor advised me to stay in this afternoon which I did.
On the range this morning.

Hippo

Now Wynne, I had no idea what you meant by 'kiboko' so I did a bit of research and discovered that the Swahili word kiboko means hippopotamus.

So, I was delighted to use it as an excuse to include this fairly random photo which you had given no other title or explanation for than **"Hippo"**. The poor old fellow doesn't look very lively, so I imagine he has been killed. I do know that Hippos posed a real risk to troops, so fair play, but I wish you'd told his story in your diary.

Sadly, however, I fear this was not what you were supervising on the evening of 5 March. I have also been told that Kiboko in Uganda is slang for men hitting people with sticks. So I guess in truth you were supervising some kind of punishment detail.

But hey, I'm leaving the hippo photo in!

A particularly personal touch – I can see what I take to be your fingerprint on the Hippos head. Presumably left as you developed the photo and handled it a little too soon.

Tuesday 6 March 1918

*Had the sty lanced this morning and it eased it considerably.
I stayed in the whole day, sent off a long letter to Gwladys.
Had some men improving my tent.*

Oh Wynne, I'm both glad that it has eased and sorry for your discomfort. Stys are awful.

Wednesday 7 March 1918

*Was inoculated this morning for the second dose, my arm rather sore to-night.
Started another letter to Gwladys.
Had a row with Gably this morning over discipline.*

I don't know what vaccination you had Wynne, but as far as I can find out only smallpox and rabies were widely available during WW1.

Thursday 8 March 1918

*My arm was quite bad this morning so did not do any parades at all but continued the letter.
Had some men collecting grass etc… to alter my tent as in the present condition it will not keep out the rain.*

Friday 9 March 1918

*Men working on my tent all day finishing about 4.30.
They have done a very good job and it has improved the tent considerably.
Developed photos this evening, the beastly red lamp broken so the small films were not much good.*

I'm so glad your tent is finally as you want it Wynne. It seems quite amazing that you could carry all your photographic paraphernalia with you, not least because I think it was against the rules to photograph military things without permission in WW1, but maybe you did have permission.

If you saw modern photographic technology (let alone the mobile phone it'd be on) you'd be amazed. The change the world has seen in 100 years is quite extraordinary. Not all of it good.

Saturday 10 March 1918

Printed photos most of the morning and continued letter the rest of the day.

Sunday 11 March 1918

*Got Turkana land moving orders this morning so had to ride into Nairobi to order three months rations and a good many other things. Returned to camp about five feeling very tired.
Did a little packing before turning in for the evening, also finished off a long letter to Gwladys. I'm afraid it will be the last long one I will be able to write for a long time as I expect I shall always be dead tired.*

Although there is no mention of Mothering Sunday in your diary, the 10 March 1918 was the fourth Sunday in lent and therefore would have been the day Wynne.

It was probably not such a big deal in 1918 - indeed originally it was thought of as celebrating 'mother church' rather than the woman who gave birth to you.

That said, I thought it might be a nice opportunity to celebrate your lovely mother (my great-grandmother), Mary Jones.

Born in the Ammanford area of Wales in 1858 she married your father John Jones in Lambeth in 1883.

In her life she gave birth to nine children only three of whom survived her. What incredibly tough lives you all had back then. We really do have so very little to moan about 100 years on.

I have included three pictures of her here, the first taken around 1896, the second around 1901 and the last around 1925. I never knew Mary, but I love her face, she looks so kind and such fun. Full of sparkle. I know she would have been thinking about you today Wynne.

Monday 12 March 1918

Had to get up very early as kit had to be ready by 7.30 and I had to sort out the kit I was leaving behind to be stored at the 3rd depot Nairobi.
Went into Nairobi about 9 and bought odds and ends in the morning. Spent most of the afternoon taking over Stokes shells for inspection by General Llewellyn before we left.
Train left at 6, the Generals brother in command.
I have a carriage with Major Llewellyn and Capt Holland. Had dinner about 11 at wayside station.

What we travel in

You labelled this photo simply "What we travel in", so I'm assuming this is the sort of carriage you travelled to dinner in with Major Llewellyn and Captain Holland.

Tuesday 13 March 1918

Arrived at Kisumu about 3.30 pm. Got on board the Kavirondo and left about 6 pulling a lighter container containing the company of natives. Did not see much of the lake this evening.

The SS Kavirondo

You are really on your way now Wynne. At the north east edge of Lake Victoria. It feels like a real adventure, but I imagine you have lots of mixed feelings. I found a picture of the SS Kavirondo[12] and discovered she was launched at Kisumu in 1913. So hopefully she was reasonably new and comfortable.

Wednesday 14 March 1918

We were held up for a few hours early this morning but managed to get into Jinja about 7. It (Lake Victoria) is really a beautiful lake and well worth seeing. I hope that I will be able to take Gwladys across it someday.
Went to the T.C. house this evening, her T.C. for the Easter.
Old Holland was getting merry when we left.

S. S. "Winifred" Jinga Harbour   D. V. Figueira, Mombasa, B. E. A.

The irony of the terrible purpose and circumstances of your journey across Africa juxtaposed with the breath taking beauty of that continent is not lost on me and it probably wasn't lost on you either.

You're seeing things that many of us, even 100 years on never see. I do so wish you'd been able to take Gwladys, she loved to travel and see the world. You would have had an amazing time together.

I found this old post card of a boat coming into Jinja harbour – I think it will be somewhat as you remember it.

Thursday 15 March 1918

Left Jinja about 11 reaching Lake Kyoga about 2.30 when we got on board The Speke, a flat-bottomed paddle boat. We had a good lunch on board. Moving off was very funny as we had to (be) pushed by a great bunch of natives; the Speke was a very steady boat and the lake, as far as I could see, was nothing better than a marsh, at least it is very shallow.

Life is still sounding reasonably comfortable Wynne, so you are right to make the most of it.

So far as I can see, the distance between Jinja at the top of Lake Victoria, and the nearest point of Lake Kyoga is about 100km, a distance you appear to have covered in around 3 1/2 hours so I'm not sure how you travelled, but clearly it cannot have been on foot.

It's been a history lesson researching around your travels Wynne. Apparently in 1858 John Speke discovered and named Lake Victoria after our then Queen. So your paddle boat would have been named in his honour. I'm sure you would have known that, but it was news to me.

Friday 16 March 1918

Arrived at lake about 7 but were unable to get the Speke alongside on account of the reeds. I went ashore about 9 in a canoe to make arrangements about unloading about 40 tonnes of supplies and found that it all had to be done in two canoes.
The camp is about a mile and a half from the landing beach. I remained on the shore till 4.30 looking after the unloading. It was a terrible job with just the two and I'm afraid I shall be at (it) tomorrow as well.
The mosquitoes this morning were the worst I have ever encountered.

Native dugout on Lake Kyoga

I'm presuming you mean that you arrived at the north shore of Lake Kyoga Wynne, as you boarded yesterday afternoon.

From my own research it seems to be a shallow lake through which the Nile flows towards Victoria, so the problems with reeds and mooring you describe sound about right.

I found this old postcard depicting a typical dug-out canoe on Lake Kyoga. It must have been quite a job for you to get 40 tonnes of supplies to the land like this.

Saturday 17 March 1918

The Major moved off with two platoons to Soroti leaving Holland and Rhodes with one platoon and I remained behind to bring on the porters. Continued the unloading today, finishing off around 4. The mosquitoes are terrible, but they say that they are not at all dangerous. I am simply covered with bumps to-day after bites last night.

This sounds like very hard work Wynne. I've discovered that Lake Kyoga is a good place for crocodile spotting, though thankfully you don't mention them here.

This picture from your albums was untitled, but I wonder if it is the lake you are at now. Certainly there seems to be some kind of unloading going on.

Monday 18 March 1918

*Checked all my stores this morning about 1500 porters arrived to move us tomorrow.
I lent the Q.M.S. my mule to go down to stores this evening and he had the misfortune to be thrown and break his leg rather nastily above the ankle; I never spent such an unpleasant time on my knees trying to put it into splints. I was simply bitten to death. He must have had awful pain poor fellow although we got him fairly drunk before starting work.*

That sounds horrible Wynne. Even though you relate the sorry tale in a fairly matter of fact manner in truth it sounds horrific. I wonder if this photo from your album is of the poor old Quarter Master with his crutches. You did not label it, so I really don't know.

I am beginning to understand the scale of the task ahead for you in maintaining the supply chain. 1500 porters and 40 tonnes of supplies is a terrific amount of stuff to shift and heaven knows how many donkeys and other livestock you had to manage as well.

Tuesday 19 March 1918

Left about 7.30 this morning with about 1500 porters for Soroti arriving there about mid-day leaving again with a fresh lot of porters for Katakwi 33 miles distant, about 2.30, did about ten miles and pitched camp for the night.
Vander Post's platoon acted as baggage guard. The rest of the company are following on tomorrow.

Goodness, the numbers you talk about here really paint a picture for us in terms of the scale of this operation. How willing were the native population to work as porters Wynne? Were they expected to fight as well if needed?

Wednesday 20 March 1918

Started from camp this morning at three arriving at Katakwi at 10.30. the last bit of the road was terrible. The heat comes up off the rock and strikes you with an awful force. I have never been so thirsty in the whole of my life before as I was when I got there.
We pitched camp on the other side of a hill and rested for the remainder of the day.
I was not feeling at all fit.

Murissigar

No wonder you get up so early Wynne to avoid the sun and complete as much of the march as you can in the dark. The heat you describe here sounds dreadful as do the road conditions – though I think the word 'road' might be stretching it somewhat.

I've no idea if this is the camp you are in now, but I think it probably shows how basic conditions are for you all. I've no doubt it was more comfortable for the officers ('twas ever thus) but it really doesn't look like there is much comfort to be had for anyone, particularly after a tough day's march.

Thursday 21 March 1918

*The rest of the company arrived at 10.30 and another bibis of the 1/6 had moved in the early morning, we decided to camp in the huts so had to move the platoon from the hill.
Major Llewellyn has decided to return as Major Ayre Smith in command of the 1/6 passed through today on his way to Nairobi and the only object of Llewellyn coming up was to enquire into the disturbance caused by the late German Askaris in the 1/6 when they refused to obey orders.
I am feeling a little better today.*

MG section Turkana EX 1917-18

Sometimes I'm not sure of the meaning of the words you use Wynne - 'bibis' for example, I can find nothing that seems to fit the context here.

You never say much about how your Swahili exam went so I wonder how difficult it is to communicate well with the many native porters and soldiers you are responsible for.

It must have been frightening to lack certainty about the allegiance of men you must fight with, but difficult for them too. They had to pick a side in a war that really wasn't about them. I imagine most would have had no great desire to fight, they just found themselves caught up in a sort of colonial land grab.

I did find an interesting piece on this subject in The International Encyclopaedia of the First World War[13]. I don't think the perspective of the thousands of native troops and carriers was fully considered in 1918. I've read about the concerns imperial powers had regarding maintaining their authority, and therefore control, in these situations. Earlier in the war there had been native up risings, but they were quashed. In truth, no war in Africa would have been possible without these men and they paid an enormous price.

Much has been written about this since the war. In an International Encyclopaedia of the First World War piece on the Askari by Michelle Moyd[14], he talks in some detail about how and why the native troops changed sides as the war progressed.

Friday 22 March 1918

Sent a letter off to Gwladys with McKinnon.
Spent most of the morning working over reports of KS inspections held before breakfast and sending a list of deficiencies back to Nairobi.
The Major left this afternoon. I was rather sorry as he has always been decent to me although somewhat fussy at times but Capt. Holland who is now in command is quite a decent fellow although perhaps not quite a soldier.
Went out shooting this evening, we got a few but not as successful as I expected. Gave loads out to what porters had arrived ready for tomorrow.

This is the only time you talk about shooting like this Wynne and yet I presume you would have done it more often as you must have had to make the most of everything that was available. I would be really fascinated to know what sort of game you went out to shoot though. As a child I remember Grandma having a sewing box made out of an elephant's foot (yuk!) and whilst I don't imagine you shot that, I guess you may have taken it back for her. I've no idea what happened to it, but I can't say it would be something I'd like to have now.

I love this photo from your album. It is not labelled but shows the 'results' of a fishing party. These off duty pictures are so human, they really bring your campaign to life for me.

I presume the British officer has a gun with him for protection, both in a military sense and against predation by lions, hippos or crocodiles.

I feel sure you must have seen some wonderful wildlife and yet I have no photographs at all. Perhaps they were just too dangerous, and you were too busy, so you tended to simply avoid them.

Saturday 23 March 1918

Moved off at six this morning for Adachal, 15 ½ miles distant. Had to leave some of the loads behind as not enough porters had arrived.
Good going arrived in shortly after 10 and was met by chief who insisted on me sitting on a chair perched on top of a mound and brought all sorts of queer things including some very unripe bananas.
The main body got in about 12 and poor old Rhodes had a very bad touch of the sun and he looked like nothing on earth. His temperature rose to over 103° in the evening.
I have a rotten lot of porters this time they already started making trouble this afternoon.
This is the last rest home we will come across and we are now going out of civilization.

Column on the march

Hardships notwithstanding, today sounds such a brilliant experience Wynne. You appear to have been welcomed by the local Chief like a King with such a fantastical ceremony. I'm sure you told Gwladys about it in one of your letters. I can just imagine the whole family reading all about it around the dinner table back at The Grange in Maesteg.

The lack of porters and their behaviour must have been a constant pressure for you, but seriously Wynne, they were so badly paid, and the work was horrifically hard, thousands of them died in such service.

These photos you took of supply chains are simply wonderful. The detail is brilliant, they're so human and illustrate powerfully how really tough it was.

Sunday 24 March 1918

Left this morning at six for Orangawayi and after going about six miles I thought (our) guide was taking us the wrong way so after cross examining found I was correct so gave him a terrible hiding and began to cut across country doing about twenty miles arriving in camp which consisted of a broken down straw hut, about 4, the main body arriving about 6; we decided on account of the scarcity of water to move on to Kiongole at midnight so rested for a while. Had nearly a hundred porters whipped for stealing f????

Okay Wynne, so this is a difficult entry for me. I realise it is also probably one of the most gruelling days for you so far. But the idea of you giving this man 'a terrible hiding' and later ordering nearly 100 porters to be 'whipped for stealing' is not comfortable.

That said, it's easy for me. You are at war and responsible for many lives and for the success of the campaign. You cannot afford to ignore lying and thieving, but you might be surprised to know that 100 years on corporal punishment of any kind is VERY controversial.

So, I won't judge you because your beliefs, experiences and ideas would have been entirely different to my own. But I do struggle not to see your actions as racist.

Kangole Hill

If I asked - would you have whipped 100 British soldiers in the same circumstances? Maybe you can understand where I am coming from.

Throughout this dairy I struggle with lots of your place names which I simply cannot find on modern maps. Did you always have them written down or did you rely on aural information? I have been trying to plot your route, but this does make it difficult.

Anyway, in the spirit of trying to further bring to life your journey, I found this photo of somewhere called Kangole Hill which, if I'm right, ought to be somewhere you recognise, maybe you even passed down this road.

Obviously, you are in very rural/remote territory and it is more than possible that lots of the place names are descriptive and unrecorded or even just made up by we Brits. Equally some might no longer exist.

Monday 25 March 1918

The company moved on together about one this morning having great difficulty getting porters from the water holes. One headman died on the way; I think it was the cruellest march I have ever done.
The porters were simply groaning under their loads, but we had to force them on as the stuff had to get through.
It is 23 miles without a drop of water, even then we were forced to stop a good hour's march from water as it was impossible to force them any further and they were falling all over the road some foaming at the mouth in a terrible state; we then let them get to water the best way they could without their loads. I was dead tired when I got in and slept most of the afternoon.
We arrived in camp at eleven.

Oh Wynne, how brutal this day was. 100 years on, it seems unimaginable. The grit you all had to show just to survive is sobering from the comfort of my armchair.

You reflect that 'the stuff had to get through' which speaks powerfully to your responsibility for the many lives depending on your success.

I don't know how aware you would have been of the way that The Great War changed forever the way we think about war. Today the idea of thousands upon thousands of young men in western France going 'over the top' to their certain death would never be acceptable. Men as cannon fodder has never been repeated in this way. These are very different times.

Like neatly packaged meat in 2018 supermarkets vs half a cow hanging proudly in the 1918 butcher's window, today we prefer the sacrifice and suffering in our wars and in our lives to be more hidden. Thousands still die in modern wars – just not our soldiers. Perhaps in many ways your generation was more honest.

You were clearly touched by the suffering of those in your charge as this unlabelled photo from your album showing two dead porters demonstrates. Two young lives ended. Individual tragedies. Unremembered and no doubt in unmarked graves. Two of thousands. Honoured here.

THE ROAD OF DONKEY BONES : A 1918 DIARY FROM BRITAIN'S WW1 EAST AFRICA CAMPAIGN

Tuesday 26 March 1918

We rested all to-day till 4.30 when we started for Moroto; 400 porters ran in the night so had to leave the loads behind. I hope they will be up shortly.
We had a good hut when we arrived at the six bed so that porters etc.. could get their fill from the water holes. A porter without water is useless and as the rains are rather late this year it is terribly cruel on them, but I am afraid it is necessary and "necessity knows no law".
My boy who I got at Katakwi has fever and has to be carried on a stretcher.
The porters have not yet recovered from the last march.

Sabakaki

It must be very difficult losing so many porters. You obviously hate the working conditions and the late rains have compounded the difficulties for everyone. I now understand that you will let nothing get in the way of doing your duty and getting these crucial supplies through and I do admire that Wynne, but I do live in a very different world – and I think I'm very glad about that.

It is reassuring that you care enough to have your boy stretchered. I've included this photo from your album of a boy called Sabakaki. I don't think this is the boy you got at Katakwi, but whoever he is, he does look horrifyingly young to be taken into a theatre of war.

This diary page records your arrangements for the boy you engaged in Katakwi. His name is Joseph and it looks like he is to get 5/- a month which has a relative wage value of around £50 today - so pretty poorly paid really Wynne, though, as you have gone to the trouble of recording it, I imagine it is the going rate.

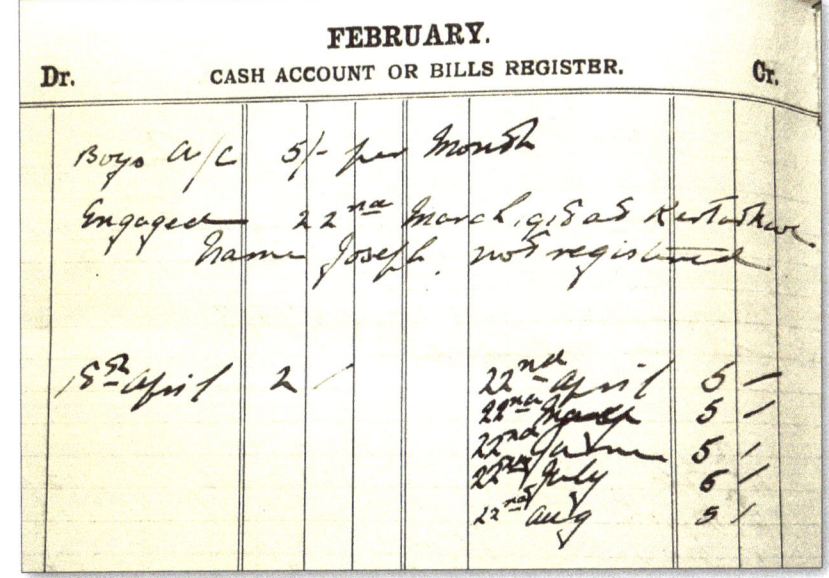

73

Wednesday 27 March 1918

Got into Moroto about five dead tired so pitched tent and had a little breakfast and then off to sleep.
I got up about nine had a bath and saw Inadfby whom I am leaving in this deathly country.
We shifted camp to a nicer spot this afternoon and then we are going to stay till Saturday. Handed over all stores to the S & J.
Moroto is heaven compared to some of the places we have come through and I expect we shall all be jolly glad to see it once we start off once more.
I wrote a letter this morning to Gwladys as I was told the post was going out at two so did not have much time, but I must write a longer one by Saturday.

The mountains near Moroto

I am so pleased to see you arrive somewhere more comfortable for a day or two at least Wynne. I'm sure everyone needs time to recuperate.

You are clearly very struck with the scenery around you which, from the photo here of the mountains near Moroto, is fairly epic. You must just want to relax and enjoy your surroundings without the burden and responsibilities of war to spoil the moment.

Thursday 28 March 1918

Working at stores all the morning and as I was dead tired, I had a rest this afternoon. Afterwards I wrote a letter to Gwladys at least started one, I intend it to be longer than the ones I have sent recently.
They are badly in need of water, everything except night in Moroto is dried up.

Friday 29 March 1918

Had our loads examined at 7.30 this morning to see which would go on donkeys and which on porters, transport is extremely scarce from this spot most of it being done on donkeys who seem to die after about two months work poor beasts. I have twenty-two loads myself, but I am about the most perhaps Holland beats me, but it will be a toss-up.
Finished off letter to Gwladys I wish I was with her I am getting to look more like a tramp every day I want someone to control me.
I bought some more drink to have with Rhodes and Ruff who are coming on tomorrow with Holland and two platoons only.

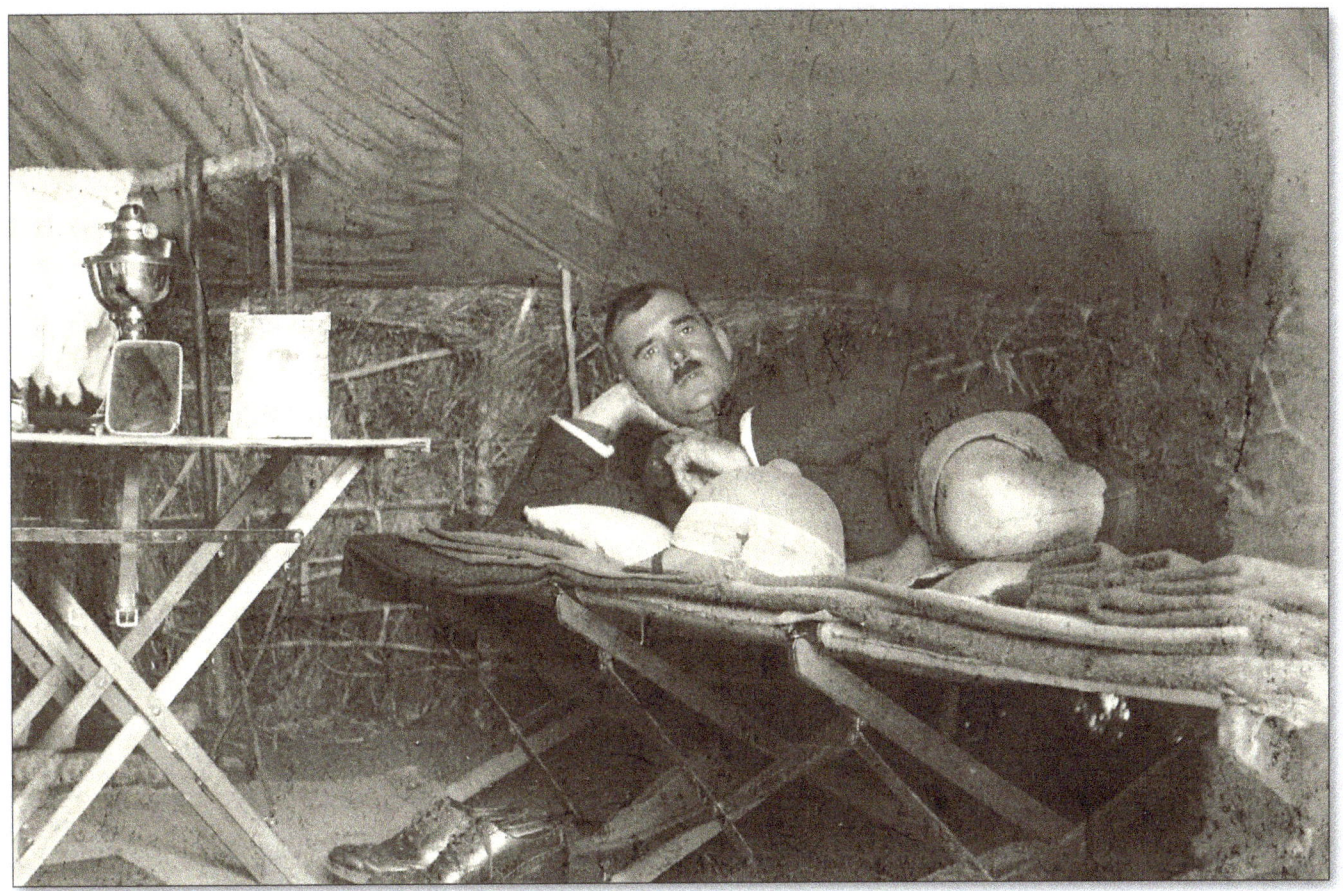

Rhodes in his tent

The suffering of the poor old donkeys must have been horrible to witness. Whatever happened to all the corpses? I wonder if they helped to keep the local lion population at bay.

It's clear that Rhodes is a good friend who you look forward to seeing. I think he was important to you. I simply love this picture; the detail is fantastic. I like to imagine you two and Ruff raising a glass or two when he gets in tomorrow.

You are missing Gwladys, and who can blame you. I was touched at your desire for someone to control you. It's nice to read your more emotional thoughts like this – you don't share them often.

Saturday 30 March 1918

Left about seven this morning on our beautiful march out of civilization taking our meat on foot and the rest of our rations strapped on the backs of donkeys.
It was a rather difficult march over the mountains and country before one's eye was none too inviting, but we have to go through with it now.
On the whole it will be rather interesting as not many whites have been over this trail before and I believe we are going where probably none have ever been, but it will be hard work.
Thank goodness the Askari's were all picked out before we left Moroto so that only the fittest are with us.
Got to No 1 camp about eleven o'clock and remained there for the day.

Lokiriama

You are entering a much more frightening and uncertain part of your journey now Wynne and perhaps, a truly adventurous one as you go into some very remote and, in 1918, uncharted country.

I do wish you had said more about your feelings and emotions in this diary, but maybe you saved that for your letters home. It sounds as though you are somewhat relishing the element of exploration, but obviously it is not without its challenges, fears and dangers.

I've no idea if this photo is of 'No. 1 Camp', but I do know that the label you gave it 'Lokiriama' is in the area out from Moroto, so it seems appropriate to include it here.

Sunday 31 March 1918

Left camp no.1 about six but the donkeys were late getting off, so I remained behind following about half an hour after the last man of the main party.
It was a terrible road going down some very nasty mountain paths. I had to shoot one of the donkeys' worse luck the poor brute could not go another inch it was dropping every few yards, so I decided to shoot it. I rode on and let the Askari do it. It is surprising to me that any live as there is very little grazing and a great scarcity of water on account of the rains failing.
We are camped in a dry riverbed without any water. It is called camp no.2. no shade.
We did not pitch our tents as they were late coming up and it is when the sun is up that one really needs it.

Lokiriama

I'm guessing that if the donkeys are struggling then so are you and your men. Horrible to have to destroy them but much worse to see your men suffer.

I note from the top of your diary page that today was Easter Sunday. I wonder if you marked it in any way or if that would have meant a little too much thinking about home.

From what you say, I think you are camping on the River Turkwell, but it does seem odd that the camp is set up on the riverbed with no shade. Your picture here is one of several labelled Lokiriama which is on the river Turkwell and is also the first place over the mountains from Moroto, so I think this might be the camp you are at now.

II b. April – June 1918

Monday 1 April 1918

Left No.2 camp punctually at six. It rained very heavily last night and as we had no tents pitched, we were hard put to it in order to keep dry, but I got nothing worse than the bottom of my bed wet.
Late last night we managed to get a little water for the march by digging very deep but even then, we only got it by little tins full.
The donkeys seemed much fresher after the rain and we managed to get a little water en route. Arrived No.3 camp at 11 there is plenty of water, but it is brackish. I suppose I will get accustomed to it. There is no shade here and the heat on the sand is frightful.
We are now in hostile country. My sheep are beginning to die. The grazing is so frightful, but I believe it is alright once we get onto the lake. My boys are feeling better today.

You are heading towards Lake Rudolf (now called Lake Turkana) which must feel like a dream to you all after such hard going with so little water. I'm not sure why no one is collecting the rainwater – at least that would have been clear. But then again, maybe they are, and you just don't mention it.

Tuesday 2 April 1918

Left No.3 rather late so was some way behind main column but there is not very much danger here although they have attacked at this part.
It is only just over 13 miles to No.4 but I think it was the longest 13 miles I have ever done, it was all sand, so the going was extremely slow.
It is not a bad camp and the water was good, but it is all spoilt by having to sleep in squares with a noisy lot of Askaris all around you.
Sergeant Walker has got a very bad touch of the sun it is all brought on by sitting in these single tents without helmets on as the tents are not sun proof.
I've had to sleep with the revolver under the pillow these nights.
I was very tired this afternoon and slept very heavily.

I'm glad that you seem to have some decent water at last Wynne, I guess you just have to make the most of that. It's clear you are feeling more threatened now, sleeping with a revolver under your pillow, but it is all so exhausting, the heat, the marching, the fear, the noisy Askaris. You may not share much about your feelings, but it isn't hard to understand from your writing just how gruelling this all is.

Wednesday 3 April 1918

The Bugler blew reveille at 4 instead of 5 this morning it made no difference to me as I am always up at that time. It rained very heavily about 5 and continued till 6 thus delaying our start. Personally, I was unable to get off till seven but made better time than usually although the going was very heavy. When I catch up with the company in the mornings, I always manage to get some tea which refreshes me greatly.

Had a showie with the Masai today over their rations. There are 14 of them and they said that two whole legs of beef was too little for them but I soon settled it saying that they wouldn't have any at all.

Sergeant Walker very ill to night and Rhodes has another slight touch of the sun and Ruff has tooth ache so we are quite a sorry family.

I love that even amidst the hardships of endless forced marches across the harsh African terrain, that oh so British pull of tea is alive and well in you Wynne. Also, the idea of being woken by a bugler in the middle of nowhere just seems so comic, but I imagine it has more to do with a British sense of order and military protocol or normality.

The marches are really taking their toll on you all with various fellow officers ailing, though you clearly have no alternative but to plough on.

My own daughter Hannah (your great granddaughter) met The Masai on a school trip to Tanzania when she was about 16. I don't think she raised the issue of their 1918 rations! Much to my regret, I hadn't made the connection back then, but she would have travelled around many of the places where you had been.

I hope one day to try and follow your path, but I'm afraid global politics mean that vast tracts of Africa are probably nearly as dangerous today as they were in 1918 and many of the places you went to remain very much off the beaten track.

I wonder how many of the fellow officers in your picture here have succumbed to the pressures of this campaign.

Thursday 4 April 1918

The last day on the road to Memerris – "The road of donkey bones". The road is simply strewn with dead donkeys that have died in the transport of stores to the lake. It is a cruel march as water is scarce and very little grazing and they live as best they can. Personally, I was very fortunate only to lose one as they usually lose many more.
The march today was 14 miles and I had the misfortune to be caught in the rain. I thought I could cut through but failed and as I had no oil skins, I got a good wetting.
Arrived in Mumuri about 11. The place simply stinks of dead meat after the rain.
Rhodes very ill and I am afraid he will have to remain which I am awfully sorry as we have been together so long, and I thought he would be on this march with me.

Yet again I am struggling to find some of the places you name, but "The Road of Donkey Bones" sounds like a good title for a book - I may yet use it.

The picture you paint of the wet, the carnage and the smell is visceral Wynne. It must have felt like some kind of hell on earth – no wonder so many fell ill.

The loss of poor old Rhodes must have been a dreadful blow, I know you will have felt that. At the back of your diary I found his next of kin details amongst a few others you had listed. I presume they are the relatives you had agreed to write to should the worst happen. I hope you never had to write to Rhodes' wife.

I like this photo you took of Rhodes, but it does make me think how terribly inappropriate some of your uniforms must have been under the African sun.

Friday 5 April 1918

Saw Major Wrayne this morning and he informed me of my work in the stunt that will be coming off very shortly. We only expect three hours fighting, of course a lot of harm can be done in that time.
Major Wrayne seems to be awfully nice but a bit of a fire eater but that means fun.
Did some general cleaning up today and arranging of cash boxes for the next five days march which we start on Sunday and from road reports it is a bit of a brute.
I am rather tired today and I am jolly glad that we are having another day's rest as I certainly need it.
Had an alarm tonight and what I saw of the square we could not hold it for half an hour, but it is not my showie, but I had to report it.

I can't help but note how 'gung ho' you sound about the possibility of seeing some action. Surely it must be bravado Wynne. You know what war is, you are not new to this, you are an experienced soldier, you've seen the hell that is the Western Front, your brother was killed there. Or is there something about the experience of war which people like me, who've never seen it, just don't understand but which is adrenal, which excites?

Lt. Francis, Major Rayne, Trafford (PO), HL Sargent

I include this photo from your album here because it includes Major Rayne. You labelled it with a different spelling and I've no idea which is right, but I'm guessing he's the man in the chair. Loving the little dog as well.

Saturday 6 April 1918

*Wrote hurried letter to Gwladys and home as the runner is going off this morning.
I always seem to be rushed as far as letters are concerned but it can't be helped now but
I must write a long letter when I get to Kubua.
Had things loaded onto saddles ready to move off in the morning as I don't wish to be delayed.
Poor old Rhodes is a little worse I am afraid this morning, but I think he will be alright in a day
or two, but he can't take any food.
Yardley who went out on a raid and was expected back yesterday has not yet returned so the
Major will not be coming up with us tomorrow worse luck.*

I do wonder what you write to Gwladys Wynne. Do you share your hopes and fears with her? Is it always at the back of your mind, that you might not write again, that it could be your last letter? Or do you just put all that out of your mind?

I thought I would share with everyone just how lovely your new young wife was. I simply love this picture of grandma, she was so petite, so young and so pretty. And, though you would never live to see it, she was also a lovely mum and a fantastic grandma.

Yardley's whereabouts must be a real worry and moving forward without the Major is just another loss, I guess. You really had to be self-sufficient didn't you. Oh, how you would have loved a satellite phone.

Sunday 7 April 1918

Left this morning at 5.45 with the donkeys and arrived at No. 1 camp about midday only about eleven miles but very hard going. Especially after the recent rain as several loads had to be taken off as the donkeys got caught in the mud in crossing the streams. I only hope that the river does not come down before we finish this trip as it will make the trip so much longer looking for places to forge the rivers. The road is very indistinct now as the rains have blotted out old footmarks and my guide lost himself just before camp.
We did not camp in the proper place because there is no shade but camped in the woods. Not a good camp from a military point of view as there is too much bush and we are a long way from our transport.

I love this entry; you are SO British Wynne. After days of punishing marches in hot sun with no rain, the rain has finally come. A good thing? No! Now you can't see the paths, the donkeys are stuck in mud and crossing the river may be dangerous. They say this is why the Australians call us 'whinging Poms', because we are never happy.

I'm teasing you of course. I can see that the truth is, this is just a very brutal march across very difficult country regardless of the weather conditions.

I have included this photo from your album. I'm afraid that time has not been kind to it, and it has become rather indistinct, so I hope it is relevant here.

Crossing the Mayen River (Soudan) after battle of Kangala

Monday 8 April 1918

*Left punctually at 5.30 and got to No. 2 camp at Lodwar at mid-day having had a very cruel march of eleven miles having had to shoot two donkeys who were absolutely done.
When we got up this morning found that syce and the three mules had departed and were unable to find them and up to the present have not reached this camp and I am afraid that they are not likely to do so as I think he is caught; it is no joke looking after a column of donkeys covering nearly a mile of road on foot and I am certainly not looking forward to tomorrows march of 24 miles across a dessert and no water anywhere, but it has to be done.
I miss old Rhodes as we always used to mess together.*

I've said before that some of the place names you use are impossible to find on modern maps, but I do know that the Loturerei Desert is just outside of Lodwar, so I'm guessing that is what you are having to cross with so much livestock and little water. I'm not sure many would attempt it today, but as you say, *"it has to be done"*.

I've found a picture of the desert here – would you recognise anything Wynne? Maybe the mountains in the distance.

Friends and comrades are really important, particularly when things get rough, so I'm really sorry that you are having to mess without your good friend Rhodes.

Tuesday 9 April 1918

As the mules did not turn up, we decided to remain at No.2 for the day; the Syce turned up about mid-day but had not found any trace of the mules so we must move tomorrow as we must be in Kubua by the 12th and it is about a three-day march.
Wrote to Gwladys at least I started a letter and I hope to be able to write a decent long one this time but up to the present it has been impossible.
I had a dose of fever yesterday and the Sunday and it is still on me, so I am afraid I shall be very weak for tomorrow's march, but we shall have to do it somehow or other I suppose. One cannot remain behind in this country.
Turkana's were sighted last night as a matter of fact they have watched us the whole way from the encampment as long as they only do that I don't mind.
I turned in early to try and sweat this fever off before tomorrow.

You would be amazed at the internet Wynne. When you refer to 'The Scye' yesterday and again today I did something called 'Googling' the term and it turns out 'The Syce' is an old colonial term meaning a person who looks after the horses or mules. The internet is sometimes a wonderful thing.

I'm sorry you are still feeling so poorly – it must be horrible on top of all the other hardships.

Wednesday 10 April 1918

Left at six this morning and it was the cruellest march I have ever done across blazing sand with a fever which was almost unbearable during the day as well as having to look at all the sick that dropped out and there were a good many absolutely down.
I was taken very ill about 200x from camp which we did not reach till five, the fever got very bad indeed and I went right off. One has to be very fit for a march like that and I hope I shall be when I do the return journey someday weather permitting, and I think I shall do it at night next time it was very silly to do it in the day this time.
The natives Sgt. Major was left well behind and has not been discovered yet, but he ought to turn up tomorrow. Lost thirteen donkeys today.

Oh Wynne, I sit here in my comfortable middle-class home, with nothing more to moan about than the fact that it's raining again. Words fail me really because what you endured 100 years ago is something most of us will never come close to experiencing. And you did it for all of our futures.

It is difficult to think how much more you can all take and yet you appear incredibly stoical about the task ahead.

Thursday 11 April 1918

Felt a little better this morning but still unfit but we arrived at our camp about 8.30 have done only nine miles as I am certain we did thirty miles yesterday instead of 24 but now that it is done I am not sorry as we are resting in Karunda in the old camp today and it is only three hours to Kubua which we will do early tomorrow morning.
The old camp is situated on the Turkwell (river) and after the recent small rains there is plenty of water donkeys had a good time for a change poor devils.
I rested the whole day, so I think I shall be quite fit tomorrow for the short march and then I hope to have a good rest.
Sgt. Major has not yet turned up and a search party were unable to trace him. I can't understand how he got off the track with two safaris behind me.

Luxury Wynne. It must be such a relief to finally have sufficient water for both man and beast and some level of comfort. I'm so glad you can rest up for a bit – and what a bonus discovering you have come further than you thought.

Friday 12 April 1918

Holland decided to go and look for Sgt Major which I think is very silly, send a search party but it hardly needs the Company Commander.
Got into Kubua about nine and it is a treat to be so near a nice stretch of water after seeing nothing but dry riverbeds. We are going to be here a few days to organise the expedition and then we are off on another eight day early safari, but everyone seems to expect a rather stiff fight as they have the position nicely repaired but we hope to get them out early enough, I should hate anything to go wrong in a country like this, a month's journey from civilization.
The stunt is commanded by the Sudanese and this scrap will be in the Sudan.
Major Wrayne who commands the KAR up here is extremely decent.
Had a bathe in the lake this evening.

The photos of your comrades enjoying the lake are amongst my absolute favourites Wynne.

You all deserve to enjoy it because the thought of the upcoming 'stunt' is a sobering one, particularly, as you say, a month's journey from civilisation.

Saturday 13 April 1918

Had a banda built this morning but they did not manage to finish it before the evening, but we will have a week in it which is better than roasting every afternoon in one of these single huts, I certainly intend begging a double tent at the first opportunity.
There might be a chance when other 1/5 leave which they are doing after this stunt is over leaving us by ourselves in this awful country, it means a lot of work for me as I have to take over all the guns and (it) is a very varied assortment of guns indeed.
We are moving north on the 20th, that is a week today.

My house, Lokiriama

Well you'll be pleased to know Wynne, I've learnt from the internet that a Banda is the name for a thatched hut in central Africa. So, I'm guessing you are going to have some comfort now you know you have a week there. Good for you.

To be honest, this photo you took of your house does look as though it's fairly comfortable and quite spacious just for one. Was it really exclusively for your use I wonder?

Sunday 14 April 1918

Everybody in camp had been promised a rest today so everyone lay around and as our Banda was finished it was a treat sitting around without our helmets on.
I had the misfortune when bathing this evening to lose my ring. I felt terribly annoyed about it, but that sort of thing is just my luck. I hope I won't lose my charms as I have had them for so long.
The buia have a parade every evening about six and it is quite amusing watching their dance and then they sing.
It looks very much like rain tonight it will freshen things up considerably.

An Ngoma

Oh Wynne, this is brilliant, and so deserved – everybody having a bit of a rest. Much needed, I think.

How awful to lose your ring though – not your wedding ring I hope. For me, 100 years on, I like to think that there is a little 'gift' from you still in the sediment of Lake Turkana. I should get out there with my metal detector.

I have no idea who the Buia you refer to are, but I did find a village called Buia in modern day Ethiopia, maybe that's where they are from. They seem to be providing you all with some evening entertainment though.

You labelled this photo 'An Ngoma' and from my research I know ngoma to be a Swahili word for drum. So perhaps your picture is of some kind of dance or music event such as the one you have described today. Maybe it is The Buia people entertaining you all. I hope so. I think these must have been really exciting and unusual experiences back in 1918 and good distractions.

Monday 15 April 1918

Had heavy rain early this morning so no parade till four in the afternoon. This camp soon gets under water and two days rain would turn it into a lake, so I expect we will have to leave here before Saturday if rains continue.
The great difficulty is that we only have enough rations for fifty days, so we are rather eager on getting the Soudan people back home, so I expect the affair will be hurried especially as the rains will bring on sickness among the troops.

Oh no Wynne. It's just horrible isn't it. Just as you get the chance to relax a little the rains come. It's either too hot and no water or too wet with flooding and disease. Let's face it, whatever the weather does it's just incredibly tough for you all.

Tuesday 16 April 1918

Got a very nasty wetting as the banda turned out to be not waterproof so I awoke this morning literally in a pool of water my blankets were absolutely soaked.
Fired off a few practice rounds with the stokes this evening the crew is getting on alright, but they will have to put in a lot of work yet before they are really fit to work the guns. So, I am afraid that in this case I will have to work it myself which is jolly hard work in these countries. Mail arrived today but no letters from home. From the paper I am afraid there has been a very serious attack in France, and we have been driven back to our 1916 position, but all the news seems so vague.

The stokes mortar[15] was invented in 1915 by Frederick Stokes and you took some wonderful pictures of training sessions with the gun and native troops of the Kings African Rifles.

It was always horrible when you didn't get post, but you do know that Gwladys and the rest of the family would all have been writing regularly.

I think the bad news you will have read will be about the Spring Offensive[16]. It was a real set back, but you have enough to worry about. Wish I could just tell you 'don't worry, we win in the end – it will all be over this year'.

Wednesday 17 April 1918

Did two parades today and did some experiments with the stokes which worked alright. The beastly runner went off this morning without my letters and it put (me) in a bad temper all day.

Your picture here Wynne, seems to show troops practicing with munitions, a Maxim I think. Quite a responsibility making sure they all know how to use the equipment.

How frustrating the post going off without your letters, you're not having much luck with post lately are you.

Thursday 18 April 1918

Did some practice firing today. The crew seems to be working quite well everything is so very makeshift that is typical of savage warfare, we have a Hotchkiss[17] pulled by oxen and everything tied together by string, but it serves its purpose very well indeed.
The rains proper seem to be hanging off a long time they are now nearly a month late and the outlook is becoming rather serious as regards our stock which wants feeding up awfully badly.

Today in the parts of Africa where you are, late or failed rains have caused famines of biblical proportions. I don't know if that was an issue back then, but I do know there was dreadful famine in 1918 in which many in the civilian population died. It was due in part to the loss of menfolk to tend the crops and to the amount of livestock taken by the armies of both sides, but the failed rains must also have impacted.

Friday 19 April 1918

Had an inspection by Colonel White early this morning and the way the Somalis turned out was exceptional seeing they have not had any new clothes for over a year and they polished all their brasses which is more than the 3/6 can ever do as they have no initiative whatever if they have not got polish. They can never think of anything else to use. They are about the worst niggers I have ever struck, and I am thankful that my crew is Somali.
The heat here in the afternoon is rather awful but luckily, we get a breeze from the lake at night. We have to move off after tomorrow and I'm afraid there will be an awful mess as usual.

Raft Crossing Lake Rudolf

I know I'm speaking to you across 100 years Wynne and I know that your education and life experience would have been very different to mine, but in 2018 the 'N' word is deeply, deeply offensive and rightly so.

Today, I know your views would be considered racist and the truth is I think they are. You (along with most of your colleagues) would have been brought up to consider the white man superior, but I hope that you did at least have a genuine human care for the welfare of all the men under your command. The majority had no particular interest in the war and probably by 1918 were fairly sick of the whole thing.

I can only say that the world has moved on and were you still in it, I like to think you would have moved on too.

That said, in 2018 the lack of coverage to commemorate and honour the sacrifices made in East Africa 100 years ago was deplorable and I find it hard not to view that fact as also essentially racist. So we have a way to go yet.

Saturday 20 April 1918

Left this morning at six at least the advance guard did. I let my gun go along with the transport today, but I take it on independently tomorrow.
We were a very fine safari this morning and must find out the exact figures and make a note as it is the biggest safari run in this country.
One thing that amused me was headquarters, consisting of the Colonel, another officer and four natives, going past with the Union Jack and when we got into camp climbed the highest sand mound and planted it in.
I have an awful mule and he can see through, but it is awful when you want a rest and you get very tired walking on sand.
Did nine miles only. Had beautiful bathing in the evening exactly like the sea.

What a wonderful image of imperial power you paint. The Colonel's entourage passing through then planting his Union Jack in a sandhill, such a hilariously British piece of pomp you conjure up for us.

This photo from your album is one of my absolute favourites Wynne, though you have not identified the owners of the bottoms! I wonder if you shared it with Gwladys. I can only imagine how wonderful it must have been to strip off and wash away all the filth and grime that must have built up on your poor abused bodies.

Sunday 21 April 1918

Started off at 5.30, had one hold and got into camp at 9 having done about ten miles, we were doing the safari by short marches as our transport is rather poor. The camels are ones we have pinched from the Turkanas and on account of the failure of rains our donkeys are dying very fast and we have sent a raiding party to the left to see if there is any chance of getting any by fair means or foul.
I love the Somali he looks after his officer so well wouldn't let him do anything if they could do it and are very careful that I am safe for the night so different from the other lot who's first thought is for themselves.
Did nine miles.

Well Wynne, I guess all's fair in love and war eh? Now you are running raiding parties to get more camels. Quite the land pirate. Your great, great grandsons Freddie and Oliver would just love that."

I do wonder why the army ever thought taking donkeys into desert areas was a good idea though. You have written often of their suffering and they are clearly unsuitability for the job. Did they not think camels would be better – and for you to ride on too, just like T.E. Lawrence, you could have become Llewellyn of Africa. Perhaps there was not a good enough supply of camels available to meet the needs in 1914-18.

This is a lovely picture of a camel from your album, you didn't label it, but I guess it's pretty self-explanatory.

Monday 22 April 1918

Started off at 5.30 as usual and did 10 ¾ miles but worse luck I got fever when I got into camp. It is a rotten nuisance fever off and on the whole time.
Woke up this morning practically covered in sand as we had a bit of a sandstorm across the dessert. We eat and drink sand and breathe sand these days.
The camps are frightfully hot as of course there is no shade whatever in this beastly plain of sand when I have finished my time up here, I don't think I shall want to see sand again. The glare almost burns your eyes at times and if possible, I always remain in my tent through the middle of the day. By the way my tent is not sun proof, so you keep your helmet on all day.

The detail you give here really brings home the hardship you and your colleagues suffer.

You have no sunglasses, no protection from the sand, no protection from the sun so you have to wear your hats all day – it sounds just horrible.

Things are ghastly enough already without knowing that the powers that be are failing to provide any of the things (mostly quite cheap) that would have helped.

Soldiers today (quite rightly) bemoan the under resourcing of equipment supplies in combat and get total support from the British people. But it's clear that in 1918 they didn't really spend much time thinking about what men needed to stay fit and healthy, you were all just expected to get on with the job in hand - and by and large, you did. Incredible really.

This photo you took of Rhodes and two other officers outside a tent shows just how poorly equipped you all are. Traditional lace up shoes can't have been ideal for crossing desserts, you must have lived with sand permanently in your shoes, and what on earth are you all wearing ties for? But perhaps that is the 100 year gap right there - you might well feel that a chap ought to look decent and keep up standards, even in the jungle. Certainly, in spite of his extraordinary achievements, TE Lawrence was openly mocked for 'going native' in Arabia.

Suffice to say Wynne, I think you all could have been a good deal better looked after!

Tuesday 23 April 1918

Started off at usual time but column seemed to be drawn out over a great stretch of country although most of the animal transport was well closed up, but the rear guard were five hours on the road.
Ruff and I put our tents over each other and it was much cooler this afternoon.
My fever was very bad this evening and the doctor is going to give me an injection of quinine tomorrow. I think I shall be saturated with the stuff before I leave this country.
The transport of the safari is 2060 donkeys loaded, 300 spare, 160 milk camels, 37 loaded, 400 porters. We have five Maxims, 4 Lewis guns, one Hotchkiss, 2 fdr and a Stokes gun and 36 white men.
Did roughly 10 miles.

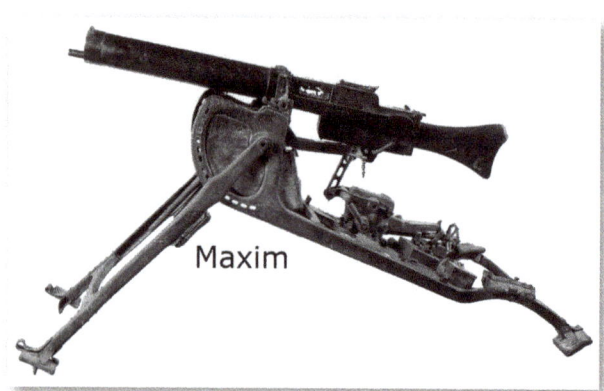
Maxim

Today's entry highlights the scale of the operation you are running and it's much bigger than I had imagined. I mean 2060 loaded donkeys, 400 porters (a lot of men to feed) and what the heck are milk camels – do I assume that's what you put in your tea? That sounds horrible.

Lewis Gun

You also list the weaponry and I have to say, to me, with no military expertise whatever, it doesn't sound that much. I wonder if you were short on those resources or whether that was actually a reasonable amount.

Also, I'm unsure how many fighting men you have. Do the porters fight if required? If not, you seem only to have 36 white men. Are there no Askari or KAR native troops with you? I feel genuinely anxious for you all out there in the middle of nowhere, it sounds so vulnerable.

Stokes Mortar

And to add to your woes it seems you have malaria. You have never mentioned mosquito netting or anything that might have helped prevent it, so I'm not sure if this was provided. You are living it, so you know how many young men are needlessly lost to disease in East Africa. I know it's no help to you, but following 1914-18 people simply were not prepared ever again for life to be as cheap as it was then.

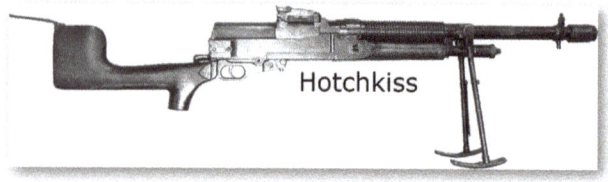
Hotchkiss

The pictures of guns here Wynne are for all us 2018 people, most of whom would have no idea what they look like otherwise.

Wednesday 24 April 1918

Started off at 5 this morning as we thought we would catch the moon but unfortunately it went down about ten minutes early, but I prefer it as we are well in camp before the sun gets too hot. To-day we were in camp by eight thirty having done a little over nine miles. Lomogol still seems a long way when really it is only 40 miles or somewhere near that, a little over, I think. Had an injection of quinine in the buttock today and this evening I am feeling better than I have for a long time. Camp an exceedingly dirty one.

Now seriously Wynne, the moon did not go down early did it? That would be a real event.

I'm relieved that you are feeling so much better, but I feel very angry on your behalf because the powers that be seem to have done nothing to prevent malaria on this campaign, unless you simply haven't mentioned it. But I can't see any evidence of it in your photos either. And there was proper advice available[18] – they just don't seem to place a high enough value on your lives, which is simply shameful.

Thursday 25 April 1918

*Our scouts caught a prisoner last night straying to the Turkanas outposts, but we were unable to get much information out of him and we cannot rely on what he gave us as he contradicted himself often.
I hope they will wait for us at Lomogol when we will give them a good hiding but if they bunk our supplies will not hold out for a longer column like this, so the Soudan people would have to be let off home.
A mail arrived to-day and thank heavens I had four from Gwladys and four from others and everyone is well. The news in the paper seems a little brighter.
Did roughly ten miles.*

I'm such a sop. I read that you took a prisoner and didn't "get much out of him" and then I just worry about any brutality involved. Of course you are at war, something I am extremely lucky never to have experienced.

I think today's entry highlights how critical your supply chain is to Britain's ability to actually fight in Africa in 1918.

What great news about the mail though, it must be a real lift to have so many lovely letters from home.

Friday 26 April 1918

Off at 5 again this morning and did a good ten miles and I was not tired in the least, so I think the fever is off me for a while at least.
A very rotten camp, swarms of flies, rotten water and everything stinks.
We are now two days from Lomogol, and I am sleeping at the foot of the mountain we have been marching on for the last seven days, but the range of hills still appears to continue north for miles and miles. We ought to find out whether the Turkana has talked or not yet.
Wrote a little to Gwladys.
The trees here have a vile smell.

The transport

The scale of the landscape in which you operate is epic. Breathtakingly beautiful and yet everything around you is feted and vile in a way that is almost unimaginable. What a stark disparity that must present, but what a classic image of the impact of war on a landscape.

These photos from your album appear to have been taken at the foot of some hills, so maybe it is near to where you are now.

In spite of their deterioration over time, they do portray the epic natures of both the landscape and the column.

Columns on the march

Saturday 27 April 1918

Did about fifteen miles but had quite a good one actually with a little shade but tons of ants but we can't get all good things together.
I would give £1 for a cold clear glass of water, since I left Moroto I have not had any water that I could even see through. I am afraid some of my friends would have thrown several fits if they had seen me drinking it.
The Turkana have moved from Lomogol as I am afraid the size of our column scared them, and I don't think the Abyssinians felt like trying to bump us at the present time.
I suppose England will have to deal with them one day and I am afraid it will be a very big undertaking indeed as
our lines of communication will be so difficult.
We think that half the Turkanas have gone into Abyssinia and half to the mountains west of here.

You might be surprised and amazed to know that today, if you offered £1 for a bottle of water, in many places they would ask for a further 10/-! Indeed you would be amazed at our feckless use of bottled water in general.

The conditions you describe here are just relentlessly appalling Wynne. You are very long suffering and quite philosophical about these things, but then I suppose you have little choice.

Sunday 28 April 1918

Did not start off till seven this morning and only did 4 miles reaching the famous Lomogol at 9 am to find the bird flown. What our next move is going to be I don't know but if they have got into the mountains, we are going to have a tough time getting them out and of course supplies will not hold out forever.
Holland and Ruff, I believe, have to stay here and it is a very nice place indeed with plenty of shade and the water is the best I have tasted since I left Moroto. What I have to do I am unaware of, but I expect I shall find land somewhere up here unless I go to Jubaland which I am not at all keen on doing. Holland and Ruff are patrolling the river today.

It seems to be a bit of a nightmare to have endured all that you have and then when you finally get to the fight, they have all fled. That must produce a strange mixture of emotions surely Wynne. No release for that adrenalin fuelled anxiety in anticipation of conflict and yet great relief that you will not risk your life today.

Of course, I am only glad that they fled, and you are safe. My very existence relies on your safe return – how fragile, strange and random all life is.

Monday 29 April 1918

*Rode around all day looking for a suitable place to build a fort and eventually decided on a flat bit of ground about 600x from the river not far from the Abyssinian camp at Lomogol.
We are going to put up stockade 4 feet thick the only difficulty will be getting enough timber at least the right kind of stuff.
There is a strong patrol out today trying to discover the direction the Turkanas have gone.
I expect a lot of them have gone into Abyssinia. I am very glad the Abyssinians have gone because we don't want trouble with their government at the present moment we might later on and then we will have plenty of excuse as they are selling rifles to the Turkanas, so they deserve a hiding and they will get it someday, we never forget.*

Making Mueressi Fort

Clearly the work is relentless Wynne, and rest is not something that is often possible.

Though I can't find Mueressi, this photo from your album depicts something of the nature of the work you have set out in detail today.

You seem well aware of the broader politics and it is interesting that in this picture, though very poor in quality, we see R Crampton Esq. This led me to the brilliant Uganda Journal[19] in which a Mr D. R. Crampton is reported as the East Africa Political Officer.

So, it seems that even back in 1914-18 you had what we now call 'spin doctors' following you around and reporting up and down the line.

R Crampton Esq. P.O. and Lt. Pinsent E.A. M.C.

Tuesday 30 April 1918

Started men cutting wood this morning. I am afraid we are going to have great difficulty to get decent logs, but we ought to be able to put up a decent stockade with the timber we can get, and four foot of sand will hold out anything and then put out a deep ditch with thorn bush inside one would be perfectly safe in this kind of warfare.
We had a heavy shower of rain last night and everybody looked like drowned rats.
The men did six hours work cutting timber and I had a lot of walking around to do to see that proper stuff was cut.
The great difficulty about the fort is the water supply as it is impossible to put (the) fort nearer than 600x to the river on account of floods but I think we can dig a well to be used only in case of emergency.

I'm so impressed with you fort building plans Wynne. Did they teach you this stuff or are you just applying your own ideas? I imagine the fun you could have had with your son Philip who loved messing around with things like this.

Wednesday 1 May 1918

I am going on tomorrow with the southern column commanded by Rayne. I am taking on my Stokes gun and 20 men of the 3/6 and I expect I shall eventually end up in Kalim with that detachment.
I expect it will be a little lonely but I should be relieved in a couple of months' time so it won't be too bad and then when I return here the fort should be finished and we ought to be fairly comfortable if only we could (give) them a knock before the Soudan people leave we ought to be comparatively safe but if we can't I'm afraid we will have rather a rough time of it but it is impossible to keep up supplies for a long column at the present moment at least perhaps transport will improve.
They are trying to do something in that line I believe. Off at rise tomorrow.

I feel for you right now. It sounds as though you will be fairly isolated for a considerable time, but yet again, you are putting on a brave face and making the most of it. I have such admiration for your quiet, stoicism and resigned courage.

Thursday 2 May 1918

Left Lomogol at six this morning. We are now quite a small safari; A Co 1/5, 20 3/6, a few M.I. Soudan M.G. I was rear guard today but although we only did ten miles I did not get into camp till mid-day as the Soudan transport was all over the place.
Not a bad camp as far as shade is concerned but does not look any too safe.
I now mess by myself as I don't like to chip in on the 1/5 but I rather like it as it does not matter what time you have your meals then.
It is going to be rather warm here as the mountains will keep away the breeze from the lake.
Did 10 miles.

Friday 3 May 1918

Was advance guard today so got into camp quite early, around 11 having done 13 miles. With luck we will reach Kalin tomorrow and I dare say I will have to form a fort there for a while and patrol the mountains as well as getting the supply columns through which leave Kabua on the 15 May, but I think I shall remain at Kalin and not go down myself as 10 men ought to be enough. This (is) not a bad camp but there is a nasty hill overlooking the camp, so I have trained my gun onto it ready to fire in case of emergency.

From what you say Wynne, you expect that other supply columns will be passing through once you are established at Kalin. I hope I have got that right as it feels a whole lot less isolated for you.

This picture from your album (which you did not give a title to) shows a camp with some shade but a hill overlooking it, so I wonder if it is where you are tonight.

Moving from Kabua

I included this picture here as it speaks to the journey of the supply columns you talk about and which you must manage when they leave Kabua on 15 May.

Saturday 4 May 1918

Main body so got into camp fairly early did 15 miles over rather rotten country. The camp is not a good one as there is not a blade of grass although there is plenty of water in the riverbed. The camp is called Kalin it would be impossible to camp where we did if the rains were on as the river is very wide, there are two hills which overlook the camp and picquets would always be needed
if the natives remain hostile.
It was very hot in the afternoon and really all this fort is, as the breeze is kept away by the mountains.
Turkana is not bad by the lake but inland it is nothing but a burning and is nothing but stones and thorn bush and as there has been a drought there is a scarcity of water and I think that is the chief reason the Turkanas have left this part. The road is getting very bad indeed.

So far as I can understand it Wynne, the rains should be due between March and May, so they were certainly very late in 1918.

That has had advantages and disadvantages.

The Turkana having gone to better pastures must have been a good thing, and surely the going being dry rather than boggy mud was a plus. But then rains would have meant plenty to drink and maybe wash in as well as better grazing for the stock. Of course rains would also have made the going very tough for you with rivers to cross etc... and I think it might also have brought disease. In truth this was never going to be easy, you are fighting in some epic scenery, but it is also treacherous - whatever the weather.

I found this picture showing the River Turkwell during the dry season – it's part of my trying to see things as you would have seen them. I'm hoping this would be familiar.

Sunday 5 May 1918

Left my detachment of 3/6 at Kalin with the survey party and one Lewis gun and they will have to do the patrolling of the mountains in that district as well as conduct the supply from Kabua on the 15th May.

We left this morning on a sort of gamble as to whether we would find water or not. We thought we might get it if we did 24 miles but fortunately, we found a little water after 15 miles, but it gave out before evening so that I couldn't even have soup.

We captured two prisoners today and about 50 goats and from information the Abyssinians are collecting hut tax in Katome valley, so we will be off after them at the double tomorrow. There is the hope that the northern column drives them into our hands, so we hope to have a scrap and perhaps catch the Abyssinians.

Caught three men and three women who say there are white men with them. If there are, we will catch it in the neck as we only have enough to manage transport.

Life continues to sound both dangerous and tough for your column Wynne, but do you really hope to have a scrap? I'm never quite sure if it is just a language thing, bravado, frustration or what. Maybe a combination, I've no idea, but you have seen action on the Western Front, you know what it entails, surely, it's not something you hope for. Or is it?

View from Mueressi Boma

This picture from your album, though quite poor quality, shows the men managing stock.

THE ROAD OF DONKEY BONES : A 1918 DIARY FROM BRITAIN'S WW1 EAST AFRICA CAMPAIGN

<u>Monday 6 May 1918</u>

When we left this morning at six, we had some doubts as to what was before us but when we got to the Katome, distance of about 10 miles, we saw plenty of stock, but the Turkana would not show fight and we were too short of men to try any stunt. As it was, we captured 600 cattle, 145 donkeys, 150 camels and about a thousand sheep and goats, we might have had the luck to drive the main force of the enemy towards the northern column but there is the danger that they will then cut through between us and get back north of Lomogol again.
We did not get any male prisoners but three women who did not give us much information.
I spent most of the day superintending the building of a big cattle pound to hold our stock for the night.
The Hotchkiss was fired today and killed three cows and nearly killed some of the Soudan MI.
We shall probably stay here for a day or two and try and get in touch with (the) northern column.
Heavy shower of rain. The grazing and water is quite good.

It sounds like quite a positive day today as an extraordinary amount of stock seems to have been gained without the need for a fight.

This picture from your album is untitled but shows a large number of camels I think. It must have been a nightmare getting all this stock through such difficult terrain. I wonder if you had much trouble from predatory big cats. You never talk about the wildlife really.

Tuesday 7 May 1918

Rained very heavily about one this morning while I was making my rounds and I got exceedingly wet as I was only in pyjamas and slippers if shots had been fired no one on earth could have heard with the thunder and the rain trying to outdo each other for making the most noise. We caught some more prisoners today and an Abyssinian was killed; from the information collected we find that apparently the Abyssinians consider this their country of course we have not been here before and that a legalised band of Abyssinians were down here ten days ago collecting tax, when they arrived here they found a scallywag lot of Abyssinians trading whom they drove away but as soon as the soldiers went they came back and that is the lot we have bumped. If we had come a week earlier, we would probably have got an awful knock.

The question now is what has happened to the northern column whom we expected to join today. I think White made a mistake when he split us up, we should all have gone north and then come south in different columns. The delay at Lomogol was (a) waste of time and we have to waste ours now simply because we can't get in touch with him.

You really made me laugh today Wynne. Doing your rounds in your pyjamas and slippers, in the rain, in the middle of Africa just sounds so very British. Did you not have an umbrella? It never even occurred to me that you would have slippers with you.

Yet again, the problems of communication are causing you all trouble and concern. How much the world has changed in 100 years, you would be amazed, but right now I just want you to be reassured. We have all become very impatient in 2018, can't wait to know anything.

Wednesday 8 May 1918

We expected to get in touch with White today but no signs yet. He took ten days rations with him, so he can exist for quite a long time, but the great trouble is that the Turkana are simply slipping through our fingers and we are powerless to stop it as we have as much as we can do to look after the transport. Whatever his idea was to split us up in this way I can't make out and I don't think he knows himself; by doing it we are simply playing into the natives' hands. We want to send a patrol over Loreniotome but it is a two days stunt and as we can't take risks until we know where White is I am afraid we are still perfectly helpless and in such a position that if the natives attacked us in force at night we should all be wiped out although we now have a very good thorn boma around us. But fortunately, they have attempted nothing yet, not even to stampede the cattle which they usually try to do so it must be presumed that they are getting out of our way.

I think you lived long enough Wynne to know that your frustrations at the decisions of your superior officers are a constant feature of WW1 in all theatres.

As you say, it is fortunate that the Turkana have attempted nothing, but it must be very frightening to be so isolated and vulnerable, not knowing anything of the northern column.

Thursday 9 May 1918

An alarm this morning about one as the sentry shot one of the prisoners whom he said was trying to escape but I am afraid it was a distinct case of murder; the Somali is a very vicious sort of a man and they have been rather spoilt which is a pity.
It rained most of the day so that if it clears tomorrow the camp will take some cleaning up, that is another reason why I wish White would hurry up and that is that this camp will soon be putrid as we are so low down and we have a very large number of lives with us which makes matters very much worse and the Sudanese is not a clean nation by any means. We let all the prisoners, including the women, go tonight as they are really only a nuisance. We gave them a few sheep to keep them on their way after all it is the best way to treat them and then they might see that we are not quite as bad as we are made out to be.

Oh Wynne, your views are of their time and will have been entirely normal, but the way you talk about the native soldiers is racist, though I hate to think of you in such a way.

That said, you have treated your prisoners with mercy and given them provisions, so I feel you are neither a harsh nor unkind man.

Friday 10 May 1918

A patrol went out today to try and get in touch with White and returned this evening without seeing any signs. Whatever, he is well overdue now.
It rained periodically the whole day which will make matters worse as far as the sanitary conditions of this camp are concerned. As it is, the drinking water is getting into a filthy place, it is alright for a day or two but when you stay a week and have rain everything gets washed down towards it and anybody who has been on savage warfare will know what that means. When you have hundreds of livies with you they kill cattle in every imaginable place and have the insides lying about all to be washed down to your drinking water, it takes you all your time watching them and getting them to clean up after it is all over.
He will surely turn up tomorrow.

The conditions you describe are just stomach churning Wynne. No wonder so many died. Over a million native troops, carriers and civilians died in East Africa, a huge number of them through sickness and yet to this day, their sacrifice remains unmarked by any monument in this country[20]. The Great War changed forever what human price is considered acceptable in war.

Saturday 11 May 1918

Patrol out again today but failed to see any traces of White and his column. I expect they will get in tomorrow as they only have rations till tomorrow night and I can't picture that lot going on half rations, they even keep their mules in if there is not much grazing but ours have to work grazing or no grazing; with all due respect, the sooner they get out of the country and leave us to it the better, if Rayne had been in command we would never have made the big mistake of splitting us up into useless columns and simply letting the enemy slip through our hands. This camp is getting putrid very fast indeed, but it does not yet come up to Muressi which is the foulest camp I have ever been in, the officer in charge ought to be shot you can smell it long before you reach it.
Was not feeling very fit during the night my chest was bothering me.

I can hear your frustration now not knowing where White and his northern column are, and presumably not really knowing if they are safe.

I love this picture, which you gave no title to, but which clearly depicts the porters you are working with. I'm thinking their local knowledge must have been invaluable, although of course many found themselves miles from their own homes. They suffered a great deal and thousands lost their lives both to sickness and fighting.

Sunday 12 May 1918

Yardley of the Sudanese got back this morning after having a scrap and having a few casualties but he got 450 cattle and 1200 donkeys and of course sheep and goats are all over the place, it is a fairly good haul but when one considers that we have to get 25,000 head of cattle to return to Sak who had them pinched by the Turkana we have a mere handful; we hear that White is somewhere on the other side of the hill but somewhat lost as his rations were only supposed to last up till tonight. I believe he has also caught a lot of cattle, but I am afraid we will spend some time yet before we get the required number; the chief question now is in which direction we will move.
I believe Yardley's men killed an official Abyssinian, I hope there won't be trouble because they are too strong for us at present and we would have to retreat as they are an organised army.

Monday 13 May 1918

No signs of White yet. I am afraid his calculations were all wrong as he told us to be here by the 6th and we have already been here seven days. As the Major said, it would have paid us to be a couple of days late but orders had to be obeyed; as it was a party of Abyssinians skipped through the pass two days before Yardley got there, of course that was the lot we drove towards them so it simply shows that all calculations were wrong and so other events since that not only wrong but the whole scheme was drawn up by someone who did not know the country.
Rayne asked for a senior KAR Officer, but none were coming so a great amount of jealousy has arisen making things on the whole very uncomfortable. Rayne knows the country and the ways of these natives. Caught 200 camels and 400 camels this afternoon.

It sounds as though you have a lot of respect for Major Rayne's knowledge and expertise Wynne, that must have been reassuring.

I've included this photo of you with Rayne and two other officers, though I think it might have been taken earlier in the campaign.

Major H Rayne MC, Capt JFL Johnstone RAMC, Lt WW Willis, Lt. L Wynne Jones MC

Tuesday 14 May 1918

A large fire reflected in the clouds well to the west this evening. It is very hard to judge the distance of a fire simply by the reflection. Anyhow, we sent out a patrol to see what it was. It might be White in which case they can direct him here or on the other hand it might be Turkana lighting signal fires as that is the way they signal in these parts.
Yardley told some of his patrol to be back with news tonight, but he is talking around his hat as the fire was about 15 to 20 miles walk away, that is counting that brute of a hill to climb if you were going in an aeroplane you could get back tonight but not otherwise, and I don't think he took it into
consideration that it was dark, and that (the) moon would not last long but we shall see if any are back in the morning.

I've decided that in 1918 you were all more comfortable with a far lower level of certainty than we can tolerate today. You had no choice of course, but I genuinely think it was a positive because it meant you had a much greater capacity for patience which in its turn allows greater time for reflection.

Life today has no space for reflection at all. Everything is instant, we can contact people on the other side of the world in a second and so the pace of life is incredibly fast with no time to think, to relax, to do nothing.

I often think that the next generation are actually losing the ability to relax. I'm not sure how you would reflect on 2018 life, but it would be fascinating to know, though I suspect you might find us all somewhat ridiculous.

Wednesday 15 May 1918

Yardley's men were not back tonight so I have come to the conclusion that the Sudanese have no idea of distance and how long it takes to cover ground.
It is getting very annoying about the Colonel as all we can do is short patrols which really bring off nothing but a few cattle now and then. Of course, the stock is picking up immensely on it and my mule is getting into fine condition as well as my donkeys they all need resting as well as the cattle that we have captured as it has been driven so very hard lately as we were on their tracks of course.
The camp is getting more foul every day and there are from 40 to 50 sick now every morning. The flies are so bad that it is surprising we don't all get dysentery. Mosquitoes started again. Finished a letter to Gwladys.

From the conditions you describe Wynne, I assume you must be losing men on a daily basis from amongst the 40-50 who are sick, and no wonder given the putrid conditions you describe in camp. Are these men simply buried on site I wonder or what?

On top of all that, you have the on-going worry and frustration regarding the whereabouts of the northern column. It appears the only benefit of the current situation is the improved condition of the stock.

Goodness knows what you write to Gwladys. Do you tell her everything just as it is? Do you share your fears and your emotions? Or do you tell her everything is alright? I wish I knew; I wish those letters were still about – not because I want to pry, but simply because they would help so much to complete the picture for me.

Your photo here, which you did not label, is in a very poor state really, but shows, something of the discomfort and boredom you all had to endure in camps. Two men sitting naked in their tent, no doubt trying to find some relief from the heat. Of course unlike in France, there was no 'down time' away from the camps. No little villages where you could spend a few days away from the front. It was relentless.

Thursday 16 May 1918

Six of Yardley's patrol got back this morning and reported that the large fire was Turkana and that there were about thirty around it. Had a short scrap killing five, the majority getting away except some more women. The camp will be full of them soon it is almost a nursery now.
No signs whatever of White. Where on earth he could have got to beats me.
Yardley, ever since he has been back, has been talking about going out. Rayne has told (him) to go out whenever he likes but he has not gone. Yet I am afraid he talks a great deal but that is all. Heard from Holland to say that Abyssinians had been down scouting around. I also feared that my Sergeant had been speared and was in a rather serious condition.
Rayne rather worried about Colonel, he is already four days over his rations.

Friday 17 May 1918

White not turned up, Yardley saw him on the 6th and if he put his men on half rations from the 7th they would be finished today so I expect the men will have to be pulling in their belts quite a lot. Of course, they will have meat which ought to keep them alive.
I feel certain that he must have sent a note to Rayne and the carrier has been scuppered en route, that is all I can think of and he is probably cursing us as much as we are cursing him.
Cleverley and Cambridge went on two days patrol today, but I don't expect they will get anything. They might get a few cattle but what we want is to catch about three hundred of their riflemen and simply slaughter them and then this country would probably be peaceful as it is it will be quite unsafe to travel without escort of at least twenty men.

Oh Wynne. Do you really want to catch about 300 men and "simply slaughter them"? Could you or would you ever contemplate doing something like that? Or is it just your frustrations you are expressing? I want to believe the latter, I really hope so, I hate to imagine you capable of such carnage.

Saturday 18 May 1918

Note from White to say he would turn up tomorrow and that we have to build a boma[21] for the stock which he said was 2,500 cattle and 600 donkeys, very disappointing considering the time he has been holding us up as I believe if we had a free hand we would have been able to capture a good many more if we had gone up to the top of Latresia but under the circumstances it was quite impossible.
I only hope the Sudanese will clear off home now that the coming back here they are only a nuisance.
The P.O.'s scrap like hell as to whether stock was captured in B.E.A. or the Sudan. The boundary is in a most ridiculous place, it should be north of Lake Rudolf and then we might be able to do something.
Party went back to escort Smith here.

Sunday 19 May 1918

White did not turn up today. I think he imagines he is on a picnic or some sort of joy ride by the way he is fooling around. In his letter he said he had large quantities of stock when we caught that amount in a day and could have caught more if we had a free hand.
I am afraid the rains have failed in northern Turkana at least trekking around now will become very much worse than previously except of course around the lake where you can always get plenty of water although it will be very brackish indeed.
Got a little Turkana puppy today which I am going to try and keep as a mascot. He is not a bad little thing, but it can hardly walk yet so will have to be carried on safari.

I feel your utter frustration at yet more delays with White and his column Wynne. It must be really difficult because you know that when he does arrive you will all have to work together.

The puppy sounds adorable though and a great distraction. I wonder what name you have given him, White maybe.

Monday 20 May 1918

White actually arrived today with his stock.
Does not look anything like 3,000 but it has not yet been counted.
I think we have made a great mistake by having camels and sheep and goats alone because the Turkana know that and don't bother to drive them away but just collect them up when they get the chance with the result that they get their cattle off at a terrible speed it is extremely difficult even for a mule to catch them. They dig spears into theirs which makes them get away almost as fast as back.
They have not yet decided whether the Sudanese are going home or not yet.
I wish to heavens they would clear out.

Hurrah! Finally, White is in camp, although I sense you are struggling to be just as positive about that as you might want to be, no doubt due to your very understandable frustrations at the time he has taken – and of course, the risk that has put you all at.

Tuesday 21 May 1918

Moved all personal donkey bomas outside which will make the atmosphere around here much healthier in all respects. We are making all porters and levies sleep outside as well so now we are practically free. Cattle is being sent back on Thursday and as usual we have to do that.
The Sudanese told us they were up here to fight and not to take cattle back. So far, they have done neither, only mucked things up generally, talking about friendlies and all that sort of rot. A friendly doesn't usually greet you with a bullet. Anyhow it is not the way I like them to greet me, much prefer them to leave that ceremony out, it sometimes becomes dangerous.

Wednesday 22 May 1918

I find it quite impossible to write letters these days. I shall wait till the mail arrives and then perhaps I can manage it. Should be in tomorrow although Smith was looking very ill when I saw him last at Lomogol.
Nearly everyone is putting up boundaries these days. One would imagine that we are going to make this a permanent camp instead of simply waiting till Smith arrives.
The Soudan love finding out things and keeping it to themselves, but I hear the Colonel is going out to meet some witch doctor or some such person to try and make peace for the Soudan, but we don't intend to do anything so silly and if we have all the cattle back and then we might talk about it but hardly before.
It looked something liked rain this morning, but it never broke.

Oh Wynne, you do sound fed up and depressed today. Unable to put your usual positive slant on anything. You are of a generation to 'keep a stiff upper lip' in the face of almost anything, but today you can't write letters, the post hasn't come, you're hating all the boundaries going up (maybe a metaphor), the Colonel is talking with a Witch Doctor and the rain didn't come. And no wonder. You have been through an enormous amount of hardship in the past five months with no end yet in sight. It's hard to judge, but I think you are made of sterner stuff than we are today, or maybe you just bottle it all up. Which is it I wonder?

Thursday 23 May 1918

Smith did not arrive today. I expect the donkeys were giving him trouble. It was very fortunate that we were able to send back 200 which ought to have relieved him considerably. I am afraid we shall have our trail in Turkana marked by dead donkeys.
The Colonel went out today but when he got there, he found that the man that was to meet him had been dead about three weeks. If (he) had told us whom he was going to see before he went, we could have told him the old fellow was dead and of no consequence whatever but the "hush hush club" is keeping up its reputation.
I hope Smith arrives in tomorrow with the mail.

Heavens, I hope the mail turns up tomorrow too. You sound nearly stir crazy. It seems that all soldiers long for news from home and, apart from wanting to hear from loved ones, when life is as tense and tedious as yours is now it must be a distraction, something else to think about and focus on. I've never been in your situation of course, but I always think letters from home would make everything worse somehow – more painful.

Sixty-three years from this day was my wedding day Wynne. I had never really thought before doing this project, that you really could have been with us, should have been with us. You would have been about 85. I so wish you had been there and that I had had the opportunity to know you.

Friday 24 May 1918

We were expecting Smith all day, but nothing turned up till the evening when a runner arrived and said he would be in tomorrow. He did bring a mail and I got a letter from Gwladys and one from Mrs Jack whom I had not heard from for a long time. It was not really the proper English mail only some letters left over from the last. Everybody is well at home. The news in the paper does not seem very bright and very surprised to read that Gough had been sent home. I always thought he would make good, but war is a treacherous game and plays some very nasty tricks on men who play with her. Armentieres is lost. One of the nicest little places I knew in France in the early part of 1915 before it was badly shelled.

It must be difficult to hear bad news about the war in Europe. I wonder how up to date the newspapers you get are or do you rely more on letters from home?

1915 must feel like a lifetime ago by now Wynne. As you now know, Armentieres was lost in April 1918 at the Battle of Lys. What you wouldn't know is that this would prove to be the last German offensive of the war. It must be hard to hear this news especially as you will have witnessed too many young men give their lives to defend the town back then.

The whole war time mail system still seems incredible to me. Despite the whole world being at war, they have managed to get a letter from Maesteg in South Wales all the way to the middle of the African bush in about a month. Incredible really.

Saturday 25 May 1918

*Smith arrived this morning but brought no stores for us. It is rather sad, but it can't be helped, and we will have to struggle on the best way we can living on rations which really are not sufficient to keep one up here. My other consignment of staff should be at Moroto at least and I hope they will remain there for a time at least.
I am not returning to Lomogol as I am going around with the column to the top of Lacarisia I expect it will be a couple of months before I get back to Lomogol and rest. I have been away from there for three weeks now and rather like it as one gets very bored sitting in a place like Lomogol of course.
There ought to be plenty of work there making the place nice and comfortable.*

You are not a man to enjoy idleness Wynne and I can really understand that. Interestingly you also seem to be something of a homemaker, relishing the opportunity to make a camp decent.

You and Gwladys would have had such fun setting up a home together.

Sunday 26 May 1918

Cambridge is taking the cattle and I am going to remain with the Major and the 1/5. We are moving off tomorrow and making for the SE corner of Mt Larissa and then going to go over the top and drive north until we strike the main party which is going up the Katome and forming a camp two days march from here. Yardley is going on our right and is going to drive across Lorusia in a westerly direction and then Turpin and Wolf are to drive south from information received the Turkana have large quantities of stock on the west of Lorusia which we hope to get. We then are going to drive south on the other side of the Katome Valley and then I expect the Sudanese will leave this country as they only came for six months and they have been eight already.

This is good to read again Wynne; I sense the positivity returning to your diary entry here and I am sure it is because at last you have a clear plan of action.

Monday 27 May 1918

Left this morning at six I was in charge of rear guard which was a long slow job indeed as we had 2000 cattle and 1000 donkeys with us as there was no water the Major had to push on for twenty miles, so I did not arrive in camp till nine o'clock. The last two hours was very hard going indeed pushing through thorn bush in the dark and I was jolly pleased when I got into bed.
Over a hundred stock died on the march and as there is not enough water for them here, I am afraid we will lose a good many more before we leave them.
Three Somalis were sent out to Holland to tell him to come out to meet us to take over stock and everything else that we can't take along with us over the hills.

Pitching a camp

What a day! On the march from 6 am to 9 pm across difficult country with little water and thousands of livestock, you must have been completely exhausted.

You called this photo "Pitching a camp" though it doesn't look like there is a whole lot of comfort after the day you've had, but I guess exhaustion means you would sleep anywhere.

Tuesday 28 May 1918

Left at six and about seven met two of Yardley's Askaris who told us that Yardley had had a very stiff fight last night and that two native Affendi's were killed and one severely wounded. When we reached his camp, we found that he had been attacked at 4 and fighting went on till 10. As soon as we got to Yardley I went out with Llewelyn Brick with 80 men to try and follow the Abyssinians up, but they were too fast for us and Cleavely wastes too much time making up his mind about things, we lost over an hour of valuable time that way, he is much too afraid of making a mistake. The Major asked me if I wanted to go so, I went along to see if anything would happen but no luck. You have to go like the deuce to catch these niggers up, but I certainly think we could have shown a little more initiative instead of sitting down and simply letting them get out of the country because that is what they will do.
15 miles today.

You know I have worried about you and racism Wynne, but I have to accept that you may not even have understood the offence of this word in 1918. Today, it is a word I would neither say nor write, but I leave it in here because it is just honest to do so. It's how you spoke, how you thought and how things were.

It feels as though you are really up for a fight. Is it the pent-up adrenalin or just wanting to 'do your bit'? Whatever the reason, as someone who thinks she would have been a fully paid up member of the 'keep your head down and get out of there alive' brigade, I find it quite extraordinary.

Wednesday 29 May 1918

All the other parties arrived today so the Lorusia patrol is over and we intend to return to Lomogol tomorrow, at least start and then fresh plans will have to be made. The next question is what is the Government going to do, surely, we can't take this lying down especially as this was an official Abyssinian company with M.I. of course it would be a big proposition tackling the swines, there are so many of them and our lines of communication would be so very long. I think the K.A.R. will have to form a proper Battalion up here and get people to volunteer for three years giving them a few advantages to compensate them for the obvious disadvantages we would have. Of course, I don't think I could volunteer for three years unless it comes very quickly as I have to think of Gwladys of course. One might be able to come to B.E.A.

Well thank goodness you are thinking about Gwladys Wynne. Three more years would be a lot to ask of you both.

Thursday 30 May 1918

Last night I attended the funeral of the native effendi22 who was badly wounded and only died yesterday evening. One wonders if he is happy now away from the worries of this country. Of course, he was not a Christian, but I wonder if that matters if the life one lives is correct. It seems terrible to be blotted out 600 miles from a railway and simply buried in the wilds with no one to tend your grave and jackals howling over you every night, but we put him well down with plenty of big stones over him, so he will not be torn to pieces.
We have counted 30 of the enemy who were killed poor devils; simply satisfying someone's greed. Moved camp five miles today in direction of Lomogol, we now have about 20 to do. Holland left for Lomogol with escort of M.I.

Kangala - Burying an Officer

The funeral of this Effendi has clearly affected you even though you must have seen so much death over the past 3-4 years Wynne.

You are almost philosophical here in considering the importance of his religion in passing judgement on this man's life. It makes me think that some of the things I have found upsetting and racist in your writing might have been areas we could have spoken about; that in the end you really are the caring and thoughtful man I so want you to be.

Your thinking about his remote and lonely final resting place is so touching. Does your writing also speak to so many of your own fears?

This photograph is almost certainly of this man's funeral. I hope it is, because then, in some small way, together we have ensured he is remembered and honoured one hundred years on.

Friday 31 May 1918

Moved on today and the going was very bad indeed all along a riverbed broken with rock we only did five miles and took a very long time over it. It was all along rocks and we camped for the night on a very high cliff but there was excellent water down below, beautifully clear and the cattle ought to at least be well watered as I am afraid they had very little yesterday.
It was very hot during the day on top of this rock, but it was an excellent defensive position which is what we are after at the present time.
Sudan and ourselves still seem to be scrapping whether to evacuate Lomogol or to make a demonstration on the Abyssinian border. They seem to be about equally divided; everything depends on the nature of the force operating against Yardley.

As you write, there is a two day conference being conducted to look at the Abyssinian question, some of which is set out in The Uganda Journal that I referred to previously. So you are clearly well up on your politics Wynne.

Saturday 1 June 1918

Did nine miles today and camped in very thick bush on banks of Lomogol River. Very comfortable camp but bad for defence but there is not much fear of attack. Conference held today, and it was decided to evacuate all Lomogol and to hold a line from Kalcha to Kaliou. There was apparently a lot of scrapping before it was decided, I should imagine that our Government will be rather annoyed about it. The weather is still fine so I'm afraid the rains have absolutely failed so we shall have to be very careful when going on safari otherwise one will find himself absolutely stranded. I feel as if I am going to get another dose of fever.

You can't help but feel that with all the hardships you and those under your command have faced, your input might have been useful at the conference Wynne. It is perhaps another example of why the term 'Lions led by Donkeys' so resonated with soldiers across all theatres in WW1.

I have so enjoyed researching around your diary and when I looked at this phrase itself, I found it is nothing new – not even in 1918. Originally credited to Roman General Chabrias, who said; *"an army of deer commanded by a lion is more to be feared than an army of lions commanded by a deer"*, it was also an Arabian proverb saying, *"An army of sheep led by a lion would defeat an army of lions led by a sheep"* and finally, in the Crimean War a Russian officer said of British soldiers, they were "lions commanded by donkeys".

So much for learning from history!

Sunday 2 June 1918

About three miles this morning to Lomogol and as we were down a guard, we arrived very early and formed camp south of Fort.
The fort is getting on wonderfully well and it is an awful shame that it will have to be pulled down again as there is a good month's work gone west, it would have been a very strong fort indeed with an excellent field office, but the great drawback is the L of C as if one month's rations were scuppered on the way up we would probably have to pull in our belts very considerably. Had breakfast with Ruff who is looking quite fat after his stay here. Gave my boys a rest to save using Ruff's.

Mueressi

I've no idea if this is the fort you are referring to Wynne, I cannot find Mueressi on the map, but it is a place you referred to previously as being somewhere you built a fort. Anyway, it's not the clearest of your photo's but I do want to include as much as possible.

Monday 3 June 1918

Had a lot of writing to do for the Major, it took me till four this afternoon so did not have much time for writing letters although the mail is going out tomorrow morning, but I managed to finish my letter to Gwladys and one home.
If some people would only write respectable reports, I would not have half as much work to do but Yardley writes ten pages about every march that he does. I am afraid that if he went away for a month, we could not supply the necessary paper.
Ruff was to have gone on with the cattle tomorrow, but it was cancelled the last thing this evening as well as the departure of the mail.

We all still moan about paperwork 100 years on. I wonder what it is about humans and paperwork, as though if we don't record things, they didn't happen or something. I hope to find some of your reports in the National Archive when I have the time Wynne.

Tuesday 4 June 1918

Got admission for P.O. Sudan force that the force that attacked Yardley was an official one or at any rate could not have entered Turkana without permission of the Abyssinian Government. The P.O. E.A. refused to agree to the evacuation of Lomogol till that admission was gained. Had to make a précis of intelligence from 2nd May to 2nd June which took me the whole morning. In the afternoon, I wrote letter to Mrs Jack. I have not written since I have been in this country. I must really write again in case this one does not get through.
Six mounted Somalis left this evening with the mail, we should get some in a few days.

Finally, Wynne, they have confirmed what you all thought, not that it makes much difference on the ground in the end, I guess.

Am I right in thinking that POEA refers to Political Officer East Africa? I would love to know how you felt about such people back in 1918.

Wednesday 5 June 1918

Left Lomogol this morning and did ten miles, very fortunately there is plenty of grazing along the lake, so my mule ought to pick up quite considerably.
The K.A.R. have taken over the cattle so we will be in the rear every day now. I was sorry to leave Lomogol as I was looking forward to staying there for a month, I really think that he is evacuating it much too hurriedly instead of waiting events.
The water in the lake is very dirty but at night a lovely breeze comes up making life quite liveable. Very warm today.

Camp on Lake Rudolf

It's always lovely to read about improved conditions Wynne and the lake generally seems to help with that although shame about the dirty water.

Thursday 6 June 1918

Only did six miles today getting as far as No.7 camp so really had quite a good rest. The K.A.R. have taken over all the cattle now so we are always last getting into camp, but I go on to line out the camp and see that the tents are pitched, and the rest of the things are arranged properly before the Major gets in. We sleep out now and it is really lovely to look up at the stars if you can't sleep. A good tropical night is lovely.

The camp photo from yesterday shows just how open things are and it must be simply wonderful to sleep out under the stars by the lake with virtually no light pollution. It must have been incredibly beautiful Wynne.

Friday 7 June 1918

Rained a very little during the night so I think that for a time I shall sleep inside my tent for a while in case the rains break. Personally, I don't think they will as they are already two months late, so I think we can consider them as failed.
Did a little over twelve miles today getting as far as No.6 camp. I expected to see Vander Post today, but I suppose he turned back when he met Hart. I am awfully annoyed as there would have been a mail for certain and now, we will have to wait till we get to Kubua.

Saturday 8 June 1918

Got to No.5 camp today, 9 miles. This is where the new route to Kalin is, one follows the river for about two days through the mountains then break off north. There is very good water in the mountains. The bathing in the lake was really fine this evening and it is a real treat to be back at the lake once more.

It must have been lovely, as your photo shows, getting into the lake to wash away the dust and sweat and to feel refreshed. That said, there must have been danger too, from crocodiles and hippos mainly. You gave this cheeky photo no label – none needed, I guess.

Sunday 9 June 1918

Got to No.4 camp this morning but as some of the transport had broken the advance guard, which had stopped for breakfast for the first time as Yardley was in charge and although the camels and the majority of the donkeys were unloaded, White got very childish and went on another two miles which meant loading up again. It would cure him to go to France for a short time and see some of the pranks played, he would be a very good bum boy to some General but that is all.
Did about 10½ miles.

Okay, so I'm picking up that you don't have much time for either Yardley or White Wynne. Perhaps that is why I can find no photos of them in your albums. In truth, I guess tempers are getting frayed all round. Hate to think what the duties of a "bum boy" on the Western Front were – probably best not to ask.

Monday 10 June 1918

Got to No.3 camp about 8 this morning only doing about six miles.
Caught a prisoner today. The Sudanese cross examined her and then sent for the Major who found that their interpreter barely knew the language so what they had written down as information was all wrong much to their disgust, if they would only discuss these subjects with men who know the country the expedition would have been a success instead of being, in my opinion, a hopeless failure.
Of course, official language can cover a multitude of sins. I hope I never have to work in conjunction with the Sudanese army again.

I know that you were learning Swahili back in Nairobi Wynne because you said you had an exam in it. I wonder how well you can converse now because it is clear that communication is quite a problem. I imagine there are a great many languages being spoken though.

Tuesday 11 June 1918

Went on to No.2 camp this morning, a distance of about 13 miles. Going fairly good but very warm. Camped right on the beach and were mad enough to bathe during the middle of the day going into the water in uniform and helmet complete. It felt very nice, but I don't think it was good for me as I felt rather ill towards evening. I have really not been feeling at all well since I left Lomogol.

Now Wynne, you took some very cheeky photos of your friends taking a dip in the lake. I don't know if you ever showed Gwladys, but I am going to include the rest of them here (next page) for no other reason than that they are so completely joyous. To those of a sensitive disposition – you have been warned!

Wednesday 12 June 1918

*Got to No.1 camp about nine o'clock, only about 8 miles. I decided to go to Karena this afternoon so left at 3 and got to Kubua at 5.30, a distance of about 71/2 miles.
There were two letters from Gwladys and one from Gwladys awaiting me when I got there.
Le Blank Smith came on as well, so I had company, but he prefers I do the talking, but
I preferred sleeping in our old camp in the old banda making one of my escorts a sentry.*

Thursday 13 June 1918

*Got up at six and got as many bandas into condition as possible before the column arrived.
A good many had been pulled down, but I managed to fix up enough for all of us. Ruff and
I taking one between us. The lake has gone down considerably since we were here last.
I was busy most of the day trying to get a nominal roll of all troops serving in the expedition.
There is a prospect of getting the Sudan medal as well as African General.
The bathing here is rotten, mud up to the knees.*

Friday 14 June 1918

*Continued with nominal roll today and got men for M.G. etc. there is really quite a lot of work to do and we get no assistance and the Major is very fond of cards and one never gets the opportunity of talking with him.
Did not feel at all well today so turned in rather early. I hope I will be fit for safari tomorrow.*

Saturday 15 June 1918

*Left Kubua this morning evacuating the place all together for the time being at least. It was quite a job as there was a great deal of material to be moved.
We got to the farthest water hole and camped for the day. It is a distance of about 14 miles, shade was very poor indeed. The cattle are dying very fast indeed.*

Off again on the relentless marching and clearly not feeling either physically or mentally 100% Wynne. It is exhausting to read, hard to imagine how you all go on really. I just want to give you a big hug.

Sunday 16 June 1918

Left the water hole at 2. Just before we left a mail arrived and I was highly delighted to get four letters from Gwladys, two from Annie and one from Evelyn but, worse luck, there were none from home.
We marched till seven and then camped for two hours. We then proceeded on at nine leaving 3/6 as transport to cattle etc. We marched till the moon went down at 12.30 and then halted for the night.

Annie Jones

Oh, thank goodness, you have letters at last Wynne, and FOUR from grandma. I don't know who Evelyn is, but Annie is your older sister of course, and someone I knew extremely well.

My Aunty Annie was lovely and, when I was a child, lived just around the corner from Gwladys in a house called "Tredean" at 32 Park Avenue, Porthcawl. She and Gina had inherited it from your parents and divided it into two flats. Tredean is in Monmouthshire, not far from the Vicarage at Wolves Newton, Chepstow, so I guess your father named it in memory of his time there. I have included this picture of Annie as I am sure she has been with us on this journey.

Monday 17 June 1918

Left at five this morning getting into Lodwar at 6.30 and of course found Van der Post in bed. Who got very excited as he thought the Major was there, but he was very fed up when he saw three miserable subs only. The road into Lodwar is rotten and I was very glad to see it as the trees on the Turkwell are the best I've seen in this country.
I am going on to Lorugum with the Major as we have to pay over some money to the Sudan force.

Tuesday 18 June 1918

Was very busy today making out different reports before the Sudan leave us tomorrow and worse luck a mail is going out tomorrow via the Sudan and of course it means I should have very little time to write to Gwladys, but I managed a ten page letter. I have really a lot to write about if only I had the time.
Five men belonging to Van der Post have been lost and I very much fear they have been speared. It is jolly hard luck on the poor devils, but war is war, even on the outposts of the Empire.

THE ROAD OF DONKEY BONES : A 1918 DIARY FROM BRITAIN'S WW1 EAST AFRICA CAMPAIGN

Wednesday 19 June 1918

The Sudan force left this morning, but I shall catch them up again at Lorugum to pay over some cash which we owe them.
We fired some Hotchkiss shells off this evening, old Bill and I firing rapids.
I am afraid a good many officers were rather drunk this evening as whiskey arrived for Ruff from Nairobi and I am afraid poor old Sargent's tent was a little the worse for wear when the evening was over. Poor old Ruff simply collapsed on his bed.

There is a real sense of departure about things now Wynne and you seem not really to be a part of it. Except that you and 'old Bill' appear to have enjoyed firing rapids from the old Hotchkiss – boys will be boys!

Thursday 20 June 1918

Left this morning and did about ten miles and then halted till three and I went on with the Major getting into Mueressi about seven this evening. Another 12 miles.
Mueressi was quite deserted and very dirty and it will certainly have to be cleaned up as we are likely to want to use it at any time when we safari through that way.

Mueressi

This photo might well be of the camp you are now passing through Wynne. I hope so, it is a real delight to see things as they were through your photographs.

127

Friday 21 June 1918

*Got into Lorugum early this morning just as soon as the Sudanese although they went on for two hours from Mueressi last night. They are leaving here tomorrow afternoon.
Had breakfast and lunch with Bartlette and had dinner with Jones Vaughan and had a very good time indeed but I was very tired. Chose the site for the new camp today.*

Reading between the lines Wynne, would it be fair to say that there is a sense of, if not retreat, then of having missed the fight? You seem quite sombre of mood and although you have enjoyed your dinner company very much and there still being much work to do, I sense that you continue to feel the need or yearning for the chance to prove yourself again. All I can say is, you have already, and you will again.

Saturday 22 June 1918

*Tried to do some work for the Major this morning but found it almost impossible as the doctor and old Brick arrived, and my tent was full most of the time.
The Sudanese left this afternoon. Officially they were rotters, but personally, most of them were quite nice.
I was dead tired this evening and very glad to get to bed. It is really very hot down and I think it will be much cooler on the ridge on the south of the river.*

I love that you liked the Sudanese Wynne. In reality of course, people are people; broadly we all have the same worries, same priorities and goals in life. We are all just human and your entry here makes me think that we might agree. People the world over are good, bad, nice, unpleasant, honest, dishonest, honourable, dishonourable – all manner of things, but at the end of the day no one race has the monopoly on the good traits and none on the bad.

Sunday 23 June 1918

*Had a lot of work to do all day as things are really in a frightful mess but I hope to get them straight as soon as I can get into an office and then get things filed properly and indexed which is the chief thing.
A mail arrived today, and I had the good luck to have two letters from Gwladys and one from mother. I was beginning to wonder what was the matter. We have a rotten lot of porters now and they are very poor workers indeed so when our camp will be finished, I don't know.*

How very British of you Wynne, wanting to get everything filed and indexed, though goodness knows how so much paperwork has been generated under the conditions in which you have all been operating. Thank goodness for it though, because it provides such a rich archive for future generations like me. I hope very much to find some of the reports you wrote and filed one day Wynne.

Monday 24 June 1918

*Had a lot of reports to make out today. I don't think there will always be quite as much but at the present time it is the supreme limit.
I wrote to Gwladys the whole afternoon and in the evening went with Willis to firm out the new camp. I think it will be much cooler up there than where we are at the present moment, because at mid-day it is almost unbearable,
even the natives complain as well as the Somalis.*

My house in Lorogumo

You labelled this photo "My house, Lorogumo" Wynne, but I wonder if it is of where you are now, Lorugum. The names seem so similar and I just wonder if you did the albums some months later.

Anyway, it would be a shame to leave it out and it is a great photo of what looks like (frankly) fairly comfortable accommodation in the circumstances Wynne.

Tuesday 25 June 1918

*Leburermoy, the big Turkana raider, gave himself up today so we have them in a beautiful thorn cage now from which I hope they will not escape.
It is rather an important capture really taking everything into consideration, of course he is only a southern Turkana so perhaps that
takes some of the guilt off the gingerbread.
We have put a fine of 2000 head of cattle on the N Gamatak to try and pacify them, but I doubt very much if they will ever pay it.*

This incredible picture in your album was tragically left untitled Wynne and I have always wondered what this immense structure was. It seemed so extreme for an animal boma, but as I read this entry I just wonder if it is in fact the beautiful thorn cage you refer to here. I guess I will never know, but it is an amazing thing.

Wednesday 26 June 1918

*There is a dickens of a lot of work to be done here we are at it the whole day.
The camp on the hill takes me practically the whole day watching the porters as they are an awful lot and it takes me all my time to finish any work whatever.
Bartlette and Dyer left here today proceeding down country,
they are taking the cattle as far as Kachiliba.*

Thursday 27 June 1918

*Cleverly arrived in with all A Co.y this morning having had quite a good time at
Napass as I believe the shooting is quite good, but the place is very unhealthy, but I am
afraid it will be necessary for us to keep a small fort there as we will have to make it
our grazing ground because it is the only place in the district where you could water
any large quantity of stock and the grass is quite good.
Blanko and Peacock left for Moroto today as well as Gemmell
who is going to make a road from Moroto to Lorugum while
Willis makes one from here to Lodwar.*

Friday 28 June 1918

*I was on a Court Marshall all day worse luck.
A manslaughter case against a Somali.
Very little else happened today.
I finished a letter to Gwladys today.*

Maybe this was just routine Wynne, but I would have loved to know more about the Court Marshall. Who did the man kill and what did the court find? If he was found guilty, what was his punishment? It seems like something really interesting and yet you record nothing of the day's proceedings.

Saturday 29 June 1918

*Cleverly, Sargent and Cambridge left for Napass today with the
majority of A Coy to guard the donkeys etc...
A convoy arrived from Moroto and thank goodness some food arrived for me
I was absolutely at the end of things and was living chiefly on rice
and meat with all sorts of funny puddings.*

Sunday 30 June 1918

*Convoy left for Kaliou today. I was pleased to get it off my chest and I hope that
before there are many more convoys to go off the assistant S&J officer will be here as
I have quite enough to do without that. I shall be very glad
when they have all been finished and everything is settled down.
Crampton and Hodge left us this afternoon for Napass and I expect we
will carry out a raid on N Gumatak and also against Loren.*

II c. July – October 1918

Monday 1 July 1918

Convoy for Lodwar today – that is the last for a bit.
Holland arrived to proceed on leave after his father's death
which occurred about a week ago.
Radford also arrived to have an interview with the Major over odds and ends.
Hollands left about four with pack mules etc… and is pushing through to
Londiani as quickly as possible.

This is a picture of the mountains near Lodwar Wynne, so I imagine this would be a familiar sight for you. What beautiful vistas you had before you during this campaign, this is just so dramatic, it cannot but have impressed you.

Tuesday 2 July 1918

Radford remained here today to give himself and his men a rest.
He has not changed very much in appearance or ways.
The camp is getting on now and will be finished in a week with any amount
of luck. The trouble is that it is rather dirty, but I shall put a
few porters on to cleaning it up tomorrow.
We intended going to Napass today but now the Major has
decided not to go until things have been straightened out.

Wednesday 3 July 1918

Radford left this morning for Lodwar where he will be stationed for some time to come except that there will be patrols etc…I am afraid we will have to go up to Lodwar very shortly. As the Turkana did not bring in all our camels tonight, we raided their many atta and brought in 175 sheep and goats being all they possessed. Johnstone and Oldfield are on their way.

Thursday 4 July 1918

We are building very hard indeed, and I hope the camp will be finished very shortly. It is really quite comfortable although much too big for defensive purposes but of course we rely a great deal on Kaliou and Lodwar for that part of the business. A mail arrived today but nothing at all for me.

Oh Wynne, I am learning so much from the research I try to do around your diary. I have discovered that Kaliou is a mountain pass about 100km from you in Lorugum and Lodwar is much further up the Turkwell river towards Lake Rudolf. So, I guess those two places protect the main routes to the camp you are building.

Is it worse when the mail doesn't arrive or when it does, and you don't get any? Rhetorical question really, I just wish you had that comfort today.

Friday 5 July 1918

I wrote letters most of the morning. Johnstone and Oldfield arrived today. Johnstone is a jolly decent sort and I think he will be a very good S.M.O. Oldfield I am afraid is a bit of an ass, he is supposed to be up here to look after transport.

I presume an S.M.O. is a Senior Medical Officer Wynne – I hope that's right. Acronyms can change quickly enough in 10 years, let alone 100.

Anyway, I found this picture of Johnstone in your album, you have labelled him; ***"Capt. J.F.L. Johnstone, R.A.M.C."*** Well R.A.M.C. is definitely the Royal Army Medical Corps, so pretty sure this is the man. No pictures of the ass, Oldfield though.

Saturday 6 July 1918

I was busy today registering all the porters. I wish they would only get decent names instead of these awful substitutes they have. How they ever say them beats me. Thank goodness I finished 120 of them today which is something seeing that there are only about 250.

Poor old Wynne, you are clearly struggling with the names. So very British to think of them as 'substitute' names. In reality I'm sure, they are just unfamiliar both in format and actual words to you.

I'm sure you wouldn't have been familiar with the different names and name formats used in parts of the world beyond Europe, so the army requirement for accurate documentation would have been quite a challenge. I imagine that many of the porters would not have been able to read or write either, so what you documented must have been your own phonetic spelling. I can see why documenting 120 might have been a day's work.

Sunday 7 July 1918

Oldfield left for Napass to brand all donkeys. Heard that 1800 cattle, 700 donkeys, 700 camels and 10,000 sheep and goats had been captured. Quite a good haul. I never seem to be able to get on any of these stunts.

That just sounds like an extraordinary amount of stock Wynne, what on earth do you do with it all?

Monday 8 July 1918

This camp is making big strides. We now have a store, MG store, a guard room, five officer's huts, dispensary, one hospital and men's lines all complete. So, we are really getting on.

Tuesday 9 July 1918

Heard from Cleaverley that he intends to be back at Napass at the end of the week. Poor old Sargent has had a very bad go of fever again. He has certainly had bad luck having had it the whole time he was in G.E.A.

So many of you have suffered really badly with the fever, I suppose it was malaria, but you don't say.

Wednesday 10 July 1918

We are very short of men here and it is rather amusing the way we place our sentries. The boma is roughly 300x square and we have under 30 men but yet we all sleep soundly. If anything happens it happens.

Not sure what you are saying here Wynne. Do you mean that the livestock are better protected than the men? It's good to hear that you are sleeping well anyway, I guess it's something of the *'if it's got your name on it'* mentality and a very necessary survival strategy.

Thursday 11 July 1918

Working on camp the whole of today. I really hope the thing will be finished very shortly now and I am really quite proud of it as it looks quite decent. It is very surprising what one can do with sticks and grass when one has to.

Oh Wynne, I so want to see the fruits of your labours here and I'm sure you must have taken a photo as you are clearly proud of what you have achieved, yet there is no picture in your album. I feel sure my collection of your pictures is incomplete.

Friday 12 July 1918

Had a letter from Crampton this morning saying that he would be at Napass today and whether we were prepared to make a raid on Lorew, so we wrote and said we could leave in the morning, but a chit brought in by Cleverly this evening said he would be at Muerressi on Sunday, so we will have them.

Goodness it all sounds so random Wynne. It's clear that things change all the time and you have to be prepared to be completely flexible, but that must take its toll mentally.

Saturday 13 July 1918

*Spent the whole day straightening up before we leave tomorrow. There is really an awful lot to be done, it will take another month to get really straight.
Had odd patrols to send off today to Willis who is making a road to Lodwar.*

Sunday 14 July 1918

Left Lorugum for Lodwar with the Major and Johnstone, did not leave till nearly three arriving at Mueressi shortly after five. Crampton arrived there about six from Napass. I have not been at all fit for the last week and I don't know how I shall stand the long safari, but I suppose it has to be done. I doubt very much if it is advisable for me to stick this country after all it is not so unhealthy, but it is nerves that worry one. 13 miles.

Monday 15 July 1918

Left Mueressi at 6 this morning and did about 11 miles. The Major intended going straight through to Lodwar, but he was suffering from a bad head, so we camped for the night. It is quite a nice camp as far as comfort goes but not a good one from a military point of view.

Tuesday 16 July 1918

Arrived at Lodwar about 9 this morning having done about 10 miles and found that it was reported that Turkana were crossing the Turkwel from the north and that Ruff had sent out a patrol of 12 RaF after them.

Wednesday 17 July 1918

Ruff's patrol got back this morning with a most terrifying that he had been attacked by 300 riflemen. When boiled down, I suppose it amounted to 10 rifles and probably 200 spearmen. Anyhow, our patrol fired off 428 rounds of ammunition and last two men killed their rifles with about 200 rounds of ammunition being captures by the Turkana which is of course very unfortunate.

Thursday 18 July 1918

Ruff, Radford and Johnstone left this morning with 60 RaF to proceed as far as Kargette to await Crampton who is coming on when mail arrives. Shortly after Ruff left, information arrived from Kariou that Abyssinians were amassing north and were going to advance south. The raid on the Loreu was then cancelled so orders were sent to Ruff to proceed to Kargette to see the scene of the fight and to get any information possible. Crampton also sent two runners to tell Hodge not to come.

Friday 19 July 1918

We simply sat at Lodwar to await any information that was forthcoming, but nothing came through all day. Orders were sent for Cleverly to reinforce Kaliou while Willis should reinforce us with the mariou. I had a lot of writing to do which kept me occupied most of the day.

Saturday 20 July 1918

Nothing turned up till this when the runners sent by Crampton to stop Hodge returned having struck riflemen who drove them back and so they were unable to deliver the orders. So, it was decided that the Loreu raid would have to continue as Hodge would have already started. Orders were accordingly sent to Ruff to wait at the halfway camp for Crampton. Sent a letter off to Gwladys.

Sunday 21 July 1918

Crampton left this morning. The mail arrived this morning but no letters for me. I am almost getting used to that now. Willis arrived in the evening with the Manica. There was absolutely nothing in the mail but that we appear to be doing a little better in France and Italy has done really well.

Monday 22 July 1918

Got work around camp done, it was really quite dirty and I am afraid we will have to move it as they put it the wrong side of the river and they would be unable to cross if the Turkwell came down. There is still a lot of work to be done here.

Tuesday 23 July 1918

Heard from Clevely that he had arrived Kaliou. Not bad going really of course all his men were mounted. I expect the Major will go to Kaliou very shortly. Have not been feeling at all well since I have been at Lodwar, it seems a most depressing place.

Wednesday 24 July 1918

Walked across the river to find a new site for the camp. There is not a very good one anywhere. It is all rock high up and then, if you go near the river, it is all sand and they have already had two moves from the river on account of dysentery; the great trouble is that Holland will certainly move it again if he ever takes command although I very much doubt if he will ever come back.

Thursday 25 July 1918

A chit from Crampton who said the stunt would last longer than expected and Ruff wanted ten days extra rations, it is the limit as we absolutely clearing Lodwar out of any rations there were ever there. Six weeks rations for 62 men makes a hole in your stock. We have now got to go off to Kagamat to clean that piece of district up. That means 14 days rations for 30 men besides porters. I aven't enough unga (maize flour) but we can make up with rice. Heard from Cleverly that he had one man killed and that the Abyssinians are selling rifles up north. Orders sent to Cleverly to retain Lorugum and to proceed to Logerit to operate in that district.

Friday 26 July 1918

We shall leave here as soon as the mail arrives. I wish I was feeling perfectly fit and then I wouldn't mind the safaris at all, but I am afraid I shall have to quit Turkana very shortly if I have to. I intend to get home as I am rather keen on getting back to France for another shot or so before it is all over. Sent off a letter to Gwladys.

Saturday 27 July 1918

Got everything ready for the safari. The Major and I are going while Willis will stay in charge at Lodwar till our return. I wish some letters would arrive before I leave. We play a rubber of bridge every evening now.

Sunday 28 July 1918

The mail arrived this morning and as usual no letters for me. It is nearly seven weeks now since I had one. We have decided to move off first thing tomorrow morning, so I have been busy all day seeing that everything is quite ready. I only wish some letters would come but one can't get everything.

Monday 29 July 1918

Left this morning about seven. Stopped at the halfway camp for mid-day break and then moved on again. It attempted to rain about 12 but it was nothing much.
We had a chance after a few Turkana shortly after leaving midway camp.
We covered 18 miles today.

Tuesday 30 July 1918

Left early this morning, stopped at eight as we got to water and then started off again at one not striking water till 8 PM when we reached the Kagamat where we ought to have met Radford. We did 27 miles today and I was dead tired when I got in.
The Kagamat was moving very slowly.

Wednesday 31 July 1918

The Kagamat was quite dry again this morning. I don't quite know what we are going to do now as I should imagine Radford is quite 4 days away from us.
I am very thankful for the rest today. I spent most of the time writing letters.
Have done 750 miles since I started trekking.

Thursday 1 August 1918

Two patrols of 10 RaF left here this morning, one in the direction of the lakes and the other up the Kagamat. They returned about six, the one from the lakes bringing a wounded prisoner, the other patrol about 12 sheep and goats and two women prisoners. Decided to let the women go in the morning giving them back their sheep and goats just keeping a few sheep for rations.

Friday 2 August 1918

No signs of Radford yet, will have to move without him unless he hurries, but it is not much care as we have no livies whatever and I don't feel like turning into a cowboy just at present. The women were let go this morning.

Saturday 3 August 1918

Had two alarms last night. The Turkana tried to get some stock, but nothing went - except getting me out of bed which of course was annoying.
Two patrols left again this morning in the direction of lake and on up the Kagamat. The one to the lake saw nothing, the other one saw large tracks of stock going south so I think we will split up into three columns and try and drive them into Cleverly or to get them myself.

I found this picture of modern day Turkana people with their cattle.

I doubt if much has changed in 100 years, either in practice, dress or environment, so hopefully this is another familiar image for you Wynne.

I know that they caused you a great deal of trouble, but the war as a whole was devastating for these people and for many other native peoples in Africa. Many suffered starvation as a result of the loss of their menfolk to what was virtual conscription, the failed rains and the demands that all armies operating in the East Africa theatre made on livestock, grain and foods in general. Truly it was a tragedy for them, and one still felt on that great continent today.

Sunday 4 August 1918

Decided today that it was quite impossible to split up on account of rations and the great shortage of water, so we will move back to Lodwar in the morning.

Monday 5 August 1918

Left today and did 21 miles and was feeling quite tired this evening.
I wanted to write letters but was absolutely done.

Tuesday 6 August 1918

Reached Lodwar this evening having covered 24 miles.
The porters were really great they have done excellent work.
Two letters from Gwladys were awaiting me.

This is a picture of me on Gwladys' knee in around 1959. That's my sister Mandy in the foreground and Gwladys' mother, Hannah Nicholas. This just reminds me how much we all missed out on knowing you.

It won't surprise you to know that Gwladys was a lovely grandma Wynne and a brave and wonderful woman. Like so many women friends and female family members in her generation, who were either never married or had been widowed, she just carried on with her life, often with your sisters Annie and Gina for company. Theirs was a peculiarly feminine world, but they just got on with it, travelled widely and often and saw it all.

Wednesday 7 August 1918

Rested this morning but left about four in the direction of Lorugum
but only did ten miles as there is no moon now.
I was very glad to leave Lodwar as it was a very dirty camp indeed.

Thursday 8 August 1918

Did 24 miles today reaching Lorugum about five. I was glad to see the
old Union Jack flying, it looked fine. The camp is beautifully clean.

Friday 9 August 1918

Rested all day as I was feeling very tired.

Saturday 10 August 1918

Had a lot of work to do as the Major is leaving. I also finished off my letters home.
This camp is quite nice although very hot and sandy.

The 10 August turns out to be a very special date for you Wynne.

On this day in 1919, having volunteered for service in Russia, you would be involved in an action at a place called Settso near Archangel for which you were awarded the Bar to your Military Cross. I said on 21 June that I felt as though you were keen for a fight, keen to serve your country again. I told you then that you would get what you wanted in due course. I am pleased for you that you did.

The 10 August was also to be the day of your death.

So Wynne, whilst I'm sure you would agree that it is a good thing none of us knows what tomorrow will bring, it is also clear that in your lifetime you met every day and every challenge with courage, determination and enthusiasm.

Sunday 11 August 1918

Mail arrived today but nothing whatever for me.
The news in the paper is ever so much brighter.
Post left at noon today.

I'm sorry you have no post again, I know that they would all have been writing regularly to you, just as you are to them, but such are the frustrations of life for soldiers away at war.

I'm not at all sure how up to date your newspapers would have been Wynne, but you must know by now that the Americans have joined the war, because their first operations were in May 1918.

Of course, they brought with them more money, more (and fresh) men and more weaponry. They must also surely have been good for moral. There is little doubt that their engagement hastened the end of the conflict.

Monday 12 August 1918

*Packed a few things this morning and sent my porters off at 11. About twelve news
arrived that Habasch had arrived in large numbers at Kabua
but I don't think there is anything in it at all.
Left with the Major about twelve and did 25 miles before resting.*

On this day just three years later, your son, (my father) Alfred Philip John Wynne-Jones would be born. Hard to imagine how much your life would change in such a short space of time Wynne.

There are tragically few pictures of you holding baby Philip, but this is my favourite - they are all still precious to us.

You should know that Gwladys, with the support of both her family and yours, did an amazing job.

Philip grew to be a lovely, lovely man. He was decent, kind, funny and loved by all who knew him.

He was a GP and although he died over 30 years ago I know, from the GP who covers his practice today, that your son, my dad is still remembered fondly by his patients – GP Amit Bhargava tells me it's a rare week when someone doesn't mention Dr Wynne – Jones. You would have been proud.

Tuesday 13 August 1918

Got into Moroto River this afternoon about three having covered 21 miles today. Had a bad go of fever which made me feel rotten. The green stuff for dinner was great.

Wednesday 14 August 1918

Went into Moroto this morning a distance of 10 miles but felt absolutely rotten so went to bed immediately and stayed there for the rest of the day. Excellent news in the papers again.

I found this picture of the mountains near Moroto Wynne. As you know by now, I am always keen to try and see things through your eyes. I hope this would be familiar.

Thursday 15 August 1918

Had a lot of things to straighten up today before leaving, was at it till late at night. We celebrated the Major's 38th birthday this evening. Mayhew the doctor is a jolly fine old chap and has advised me a rest of a week, to be fed up with cream and green food.

Friday 16 August 1918

The Major left this morning. I was very sorry to see him go as he has been awfully decent to me the whole time I have been up here. Rested this afternoon.

Saturday 17 August 1918

Left for Moroto River this morning where I am going to build a camp and have a rest. Rode back with a spear made for Mayhew who is coming out here tomorrow. Slept at Moroto. 20 miles.

Sunday 18 August 1918

*Rode out with Mayhew arriving at the river in time for lunch.
Walked up the hill this afternoon. Feeling much fitter. 12 miles.*

Monday 19 August 1918

*Marked out camp and started building. The porters are new ones and
inexperienced, so I am afraid it will be a slow job.
Tollerello taken ill today so Mayhew did not leave as he intended to do.*

Tuesday 20 August 1918

*Not feeling very fit I am afraid my neck is going to worry me again
which is a nuisance but can't be helped.
Continued building today and sent off a mail.*

Wednesday 21 August 1918

*Still feeling rotten. As Holland is on the way
have decided to wait here for him before going to Lorugum.*

Thursday 22 August 1918

*Got up feeling quite ill this morning. Had an accident this evening and injured my neck.
Mayhew seemed to think it had cracked, of course I knew
nothing of it at the time, but I was told I was very sick all that night.*

I think you have a weakness in your neck Wynne, which may have made this injury worse for you. You were injured on 2 April 1916 while on patrol at a place called Ferme du Bois on the Western Front. I was always told that they tried unsuccessfully to surgically remove some shrapnel in your neck via your mouth. I think it would have been sufficient for you not to return to active service, but, of course, that wouldn't have been you would it.

Friday 23 August 1918

*I am in sandbags today or at least bags of porto and I will have to remain like this for a
fortnight. Felt rotten all day, especially at night.*

Saturday 24 August 1918

*Sargent arrived down today to help Mayhew.
I feel like nothing on earth and not able to write.*

Sunday 25 August 1918

Rotten night, a little better today.
Hope I will be able to write a letter to Gwladys but doubt it.

Monday 26 August 1918

Little better but unable to write.
Mail ought to be in tomorrow. I only hope.

Tuesday 27 August 1918

Head rather painful today.
Got Gemmel to write to Gwladys.

You took this photo much earlier in the campaign I think Wynne, maybe in Nairobi, but it is nice to be able to put faces to names, especially as dear Gemmel is being so kind to you now.

As though life in Africa wasn't bad enough already being confined to bed in the heat and discomfort, being so very far from medical help and comfort must have been both dreadful and frightening for you. I can only hope you feel better soon.

Lt W Gemmell K.A.R.

Wednesday 28 August 1918

My bags, dogs and all my kit arrived from Lorugum today.
Mail arrived in the evening but nothing for me.
Good news in papers.

Thursday 29 August 1918

Very painful today and I am afraid I shall be in bed for some time yet.

Friday 30 August 1918

Heard that Johnstone will be down shortly to evacuate me out of Turkana.
Sargent is to take me down.

Saturday 31 August 1918

Had a bad night last night so am feeling rotten.

Sunday 1 September 1918

A little better but neck is still painful.

Monday 2 September 1918

Johnstone arrived today and tells me that I shall be in bed at least another three weeks worse luck.

Tuesday 3 September 1918

Got Sargent to write to Gwladys today as I am still unable.

Wednesday 4 September 1918

A good mail arrived in today seven from Gwladys and two from home they have bucked me up tremendously. News in the paper is excellent.

Thursday 5 September 1918

Johnstone came on duty tonight poor Mayhew was dead tired as he has had a good fortnight of it. Read my letters.

Friday 6 September 1918

Reread all my letters. Have a slight headache and temperature today.

Saturday 7 September 1918

Read a little today but I don't read much as it hurts my eyes.

Sunday 8 September 1918

Still flat on my back but am feeling much better although I can't eat much.

Monday 9 September 1918

Mayhew allowed me to sit up on an extra pillow so that I could write to Gwladys. I started a short note.

Tuesday 10 September 1918

*Finished off a note to Gwladys. I do hope she won't worry about
me because I am getting better.*

Wednesday 11 September 1918

*Given an extra pillow today so am feeling highly packed although it
feels queer to have my head up.
Mail today but no letters.*

Thursday 12 September 1918

*Was moved into a new banda this evening and really it is a great improvement.
The other one was very old, and things were falling off the roof.*

Friday 13 September 1918

I have a bit of a head today; I only wish I could get to a hospital.

Saturday 14 September 1918

*Allowed to sit up in bed for first time, got my boys to make a
bed rest but am feeling very feeble.*

Sunday 15 September 1918

*Still sitting up in bed but not feeling quite so well as I am afraid
I strained my neck slightly last night.
Wrote to Gwladys.*

Monday 16 September 1918

*Mayhew left for Lodwar this afternoon. I am awfully sorry
because he has really looked after me very well indeed.
Got up a little today.*

Tuesday 17 September 1918

*Rhodes arrived today looking very fit,
but I don't think he will stand it and Johnstone thinks the same.
He tells me that Edric is missing, I hope he is safe at least.*

Wednesday 18 September 1918

*Tollesello arrived from Lorugum today looking quite ill. He never was fit, and I expect his turn will soon come. He says that both Cleverly and Keiser are rather sandy.
Expected mail today but nothing doing.*

Thursday 19 September 1918

*As I had a slight attack last night, I had to stay in bed today but am feeling much better except that my head feels quite numb.
Gemmel left this morning for Nairobi. He is being invalided out of Turkana.*

Friday 20 September 1918

*The mail arrived today but nothing for me. I cannot understand as everyone has had letters up to July 5th from England and my last is May 15th.
I finished photos today for my collection of Turkana.
Up again today.*

I don't know how complete the collection of photos I have is Wynne. Do you refer to the photos of the Turkana Patrol campaign here, in which case they may be what I have. I certainly have none of the colour photos you talked of earlier and it is such a shame to have lost them.

Saturday 21 September 1918

*Prepared my stretcher today for my journey south. I am afraid it will be rather uncomfortable, but Sargent did as much as he could.
Wrote a few letters.*

Sunday 22 September 1918

My head is simply jumping today. I hope it will get better shortly especially as I have to leave on Thursday.

Monday 23 September 1918

Ruff arrived this morning looking very fit, but I believe his teeth are worrying him quite a lot, so he will be coming down tomorrow.

Tuesday 24 September 1918

Donkeys and porters left about ten, so I had lunch with old Bill and left about 2.30 arriving Moroto 6.15 having done 10 miles but the hood over the stretcher broke down several times then delaying me considerably. A stretcher is an awful thing to travel in over rough country.

Oh this sounds dreadful Wynne. On the face of it being carried sounds better but it really isn't is it.

Wednesday 25 September 1918

Left Moroto at 2 on a native bed which is much better than a stretcher. Got to Alali at 6.15, a distance of 14 miles, feeling tired when I got into camp.

Thursday 26 September 1918

A short march today to Bokora, only 8 miles so had a fairly good rest. Hurt my neck slightly this evening. Johnstone is sending the mail after me, so I hope it will arrive tomorrow.

Friday 27 September 1918

Left Bokora very early but got held up on the road as I had a slight attack so did not get into camp till one having done 15 miles; water very bad at this camp; Orang Wazi

Saturday 28 September 1918

Left this morning at 5.30 and got to Adachal at 3 having done 21 miles, two miles out of Adachal an awful storm broke and I got very wet indeed. Very tired.

Poor Wynne, you are having such a rotten time and it must be quite anti-climactic coming out as you are.

Sunday 29 September 1918

Left Adachal 5.30, arrived Katakwi K.A.R. House at 11,
a distance of 17 miles having stopped for breakfast on the road.
We are changing porters here and going on tomorrow.

Goodness you must have been relieved to find some comfort in the KAR house Wynne.

Monday 30 September 1918

Left Katakwi at 5 and did 12 miles to Lowera, a rotten camp,
only a native bunch.

Sometimes I really wish you had added more detail Wynne. What on earth is a "native Brunch" I wonder.

Tuesday 1 October 1918

Left at 5 and did 16 miles to Soroti.
It was a treat to get to a decent camp and had a respectable house for a change.

I wonder if you mean a conventional house or a hut Wynne. Either way if you view it as respectable, I imagine it holds some comfort and I am so very glad for that. You have all had such a gruelling time of it.

Wednesday 2 October 1918

Rested most of the day except for buying a few things this morning.

Thursday 3 October 1918

I was married a year ago today and it is one of the things I will never regret.

I'm so glad you remembered Wynne. What a disaster it would have been had you not. This picture of that happy day has been hanging on my lounge wall for as long as I can remember, but I'm afraid I still don't know who everyone is.

Anyway, this is the best I can do:
Back Row (L to R):
Gwyn Nicholas (bride's brother), Gwyn's wife, Best Man, Wynne, Gwladys, Brenda Griffiths (friend of bride), Mary (bride's maternal aunt), Mary's husband.
Front Row (L to R):
The vicar, Annie Jones (groom's older sister), Alfred Nicholas (bride's father), Kitty (bride's cousin and Mary's daughter), Cedric (bride's brother), Hannah Nicholas (bride's mother), Rev. John Jones (groom's father), Ivor Nicholas (bride's brother).

You are all on the lawn at The Grange, Neath Road, Maesteg. I can remember that fence from my early childhood and close observers will note it is the backdrop for many photographs in this book, including the cover.

Friday 4 October 1918

Watched some tennis this evening. Had another attack last night.

Saturday 5 October 1918

Sent the loads off for Lalle this morning. Had lunch with Mr & Mrs Taylor and then went to Lalle, 12 miles. Arrived 5.30 and found that the boat had not arrived.

Sunday 6 October 1918

Had a very restless night lasting and as it came on to rain, so we had to move our bed into a shed in which cows were stabled.

Monday 7 October 1918

Slept there in a hut of 9' x 9' last night and was rather a squash. The boat arrived about 10 but it was raining very hard so after getting very wet we turned back into bed.

Tuesday 8 October 1918

Got out at 1 am and got to the boat – S.S. Stanley. Left Lalle at 2am arrived Mumias and got at 2pm had dinner on board then left at 9.30 pm

This a picture I found of the fine steamer the SS Stanley, I simply love finding images of the things you talk about. Of course it will have been named after the great explorer.

Wednesday 9 October 1918

*Arrived Jinja at 2 am lift by S.S. Clement Hill at 2.30.
Had another attack this evening.*

This is a rather grainy image of the S.S. Clement Hill.

She was a cargo ship on Lake Victoria and in 1908 had a rather special passenger. Winston S. Churchill[23] sailed on her in 1908 in his capacity as visiting Secretary of State for the Colonies and he said:

'I woke the next morning to find myself afloat on a magnificent ship. Its long and spacious decks are as snowy as those of a pleasure yacht. It is equipped with baths, electric light, and all modern necessities. There is an excellent table, also a well-selected library. Smart blue-jackets with ebony faces are polishing the brass work, dapper white-clad British naval officers pace the bridge. We are steaming at ten knots across an immense sea of fresh water as big as Scotland, lifted higher than the summit of Ben Nevis. At times we are a complete circle of lake and sky, without a sign of land . . . the air is cool and fresh and the scenery splendid, and yet our route crosses the equator.'

I hope your comparatively brief time on board the St Clement was as comfortable as Winston's Wynne because you are really suffering now, and both need and deserve some real cossetting I feel.

Thursday 10 October 1918

Arrived Kisamu at 9am left 4.30.
Had dinner at Muhoroni.

You are so nearly there, back in civilisation as you put it. What a terrible time you have had in the past weeks coming out of the bush. I am so relieved for you as your safe return now feels certain and they can help you with the pain you have had to endure.

This may all be rather fanciful on my part but I'm really wishing you some comfort on your long journey back to South Wales.

Friday 11 October 1918

Very cold last night. Had breakfast at Kajabi.

And it is here that you 'sign off' Wynne.

I don't know what happened next or how your still long journey home went, but you are back in civilisation now with access to the medical care you need. Quite why you wrote no more I will never know, perhaps you just weren't up to it or perhaps you just felt your Africa adventure was effectively over. Whatever the reason it is our loss today.

I feel like I have been on a journey with you, one I really didn't expect to take in 2018. It has been both an education and a privilege to get to know you in such an unexpected way.

Of course, I wish I had actually known you and we could have talked about all of this because there are just so very many unanswered questions. The truth is though that given the age gap between us, your generations reticence to talk about these things and simply the realities of life, I probably wouldn't have shown any interest and you probably wouldn't have pushed it. Such a shame.

I am so very proud of what you achieved in such a short life Wynne. So please forgive me if I continue to 'show off' a bit for you here. I want to share with anyone who might care to read this story, all that I know about the next part of your life. Brief as it was to be, your contribution is far from over and what I know of that contribution, I am going to share here.

So thank you, Wynne you should know that it has been a real pleasure.

THE ROAD OF DONKEY BONES : A 1918 DIARY FROM BRITAIN'S WW1 EAST AFRICA CAMPAIGN

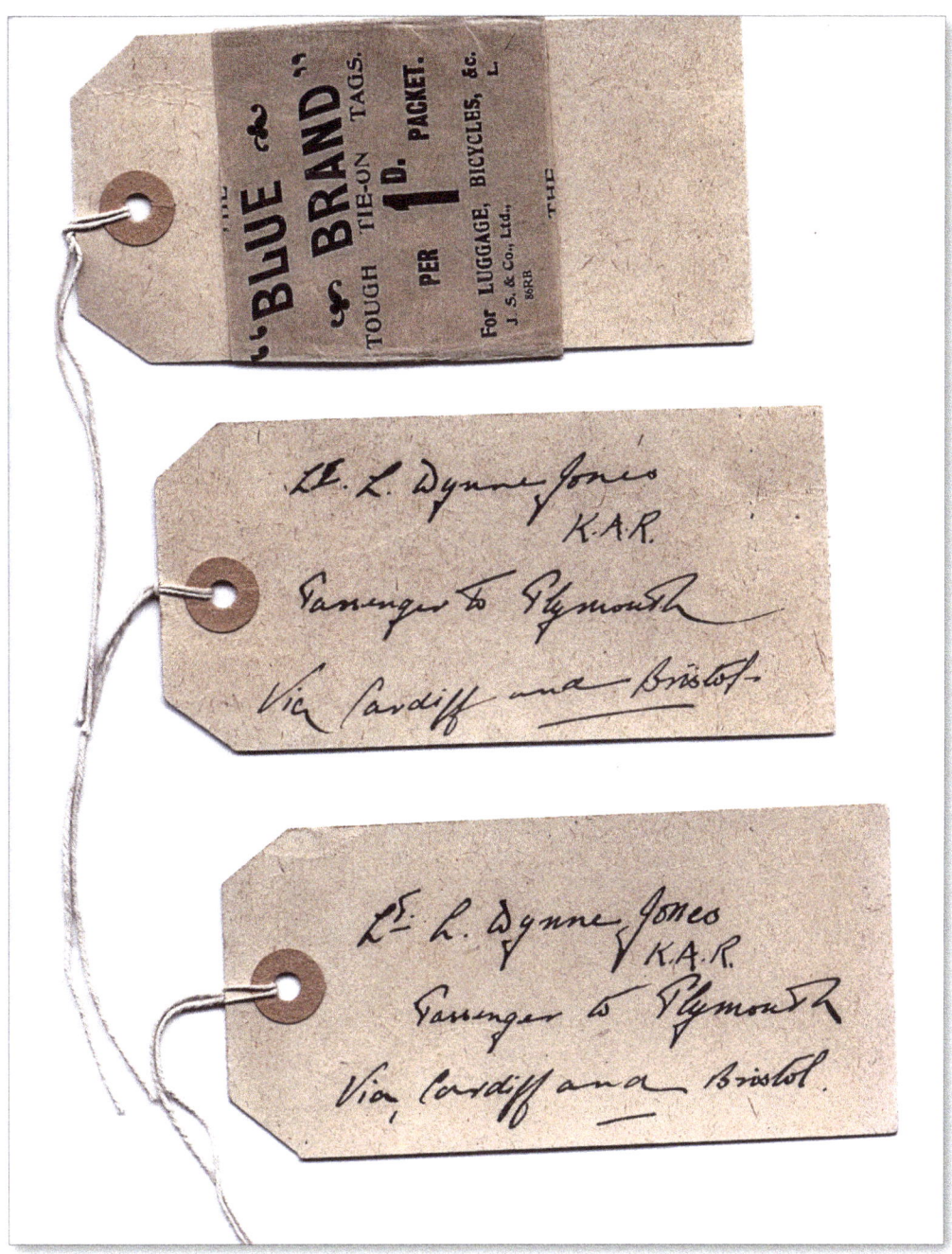

The final picture in the diary section here is of Wynne's luggage labels for his trip home.

As you have already read, my grandfather wrote no more about his journey back to his South Wales home, but these luggage labels suggest that he went first to Tangier where I presume, he boarded a ship bound for Plymouth via Bristol and Cardiff. I would assume he disembarked at Cardiff.

The labels are written in Wynne's own hand and have clearly not been used, so I guess were surplus to requirements.

Unsurprising that he kept them though. I don't quite know why, but I find them very personal items.

PART III

1918 – 1922

Life and Death After the War

III a. Russia

After returning from Africa, and presumably celebrating the end of the Great War with his family and friends in Maesteg, Wynne remained in the Royal Welch Fusiliers.

I think for anyone reading this diary, it must be clear how keen Wynne has been to 'prove' himself again in the service of his country. It's a sort of nobleness that I'm not sure is as common today as it might have been then, but my grandfather's desire to be involved in more action is absolutely clear throughout his diary.

His family and his young wife Gwladys in particular, must have been so relieved and delighted to have Wynne safely home when so many young men either never returned or returned badly injured. Indeed, they had experienced both injury and death within their own family. So, I have always felt it must have been very painful for them all when, in April of 1919, while attached to the 45th Battalion Royal Fusiliers, having volunteered, Wynne embarked for Archangel in Russia where the British were involved in the continued fighting against the Bolsheviks following the Russian revolution.

So grandfather did see action again and was able to prove his gallantry during an operation in a place called Settso near Archangel, Russia for which he was awarded the bar to his Military Cross.

The citation, although dated 21 August 1919, was awarded for conspicuous gallantry and devotion to duty during an attack on Settso on 10th Aug 1919. The valour shown on this day has a poignant irony given that it would be exactly two years later on 10th August 1921 that Wynne would so tragically lose his own life at the age of just 26.

The citation, a reproduction of which is on the next page, was handwritten and signed by Major General Edmund Ironside, Commander Allied Forces, Archangel.

RESEARCHED AND COMPILED BY ALISON CORNELL

> General Headquarters
> Allied Forces. Archangel.
> 21st August. 1919.
>
> By virtue of the authority which has been extended to me by His Britannic Majesty's Government, I hereby have the honour of conferring upon you:—
>
> Lieut. Llewellyn Wynne Jones. M.C.,
>   The. Royal. Welch. Fusiliers.
>   attached 45th Bn Royal Fusiliers.
>
> the "Bar to the Military Cross" in recognition of your gallant conduct. The following is the official account of your conduct for which the award has been made:—
>
> "For conspicuous gallantry & devotion to duty. This officer during the recent operations was conspicuous for his untiring energy & pluck during the attack on SELTSO. He personally scouted the defences prior to the attack, & during the action was cool & resourceful throughout, & although he was in a very dangerous situation being nearly surrounded by the enemy he withdrew his men bringing out all his casualties. His conduct throughout was deserving of the highest praise, & his personal disregard of danger under heavy & well-directed fire was a splendid example to all ranks. On previous occasions this officer has shewn marked gallantry & initiative when on patrol."

The handwritten citation for the Bar to grandfathers Military Cross

> I heartily congratulate you upon the honour which has thus been conferred upon you.
>
> E. Ironside.
>
> Major. General
> General Officer. Commanding Allied Forces
> Archangel.

General Headquarters
Allied Forces
Archangel

21st August 1919

By virtue of the authority which has been extended to me by His Britannic Majesty's Government, I hereby have the honour of conferring upon you -

Lieutenant Llewellyn Wynne Jones M.C.,
The Royal Welch Fusiliers
attached 45th Bn. Royal Fusiliers

the "Bar to the Military Cross"
in recognition of your gallant conduct.

The following is the official account of your conduct for which the award has been made: -

"For conspicuous gallantry and devotion to duty. This officer during recent operations was conspicuous for his untiring energy and pluck during the attack on Settso. He personally scouted the defences prior to the attack, and during the action was cool and resourceful throughout, and although he was in a very dangerous situation, being nearly surrounded by the enemy, he withdrew his men bringing out all his casualties. His conduct throughout was deserving of the highest praise, and his personal disregard of danger under heavy and well directed fire was a splendid example to all ranks. On previous occasions this officer has shown marked gallantry and initiative when on patrol."

I hereby congratulate you upon the honour which has thus been conferred upon you.

E. Ironside
Major General

General Officer Commanding Allied Forces
Archangel

III b. Home Life, Work Life & Territorial Army Unit

The Grange, Maesteg

Once Wynne returned from Russia, the war was of course all over, and he began to settle back into civilian life.

He and Gwladys were living with her parents, Alfred and Hannah Nicholas at The Grange on the Neath Road in Maesteg.

At the outbreak of war back in 1914, Wynne had been articled as a Clerk to Rufus Redmond Earle, a Barrister of the Supreme Court of Saskatchewan with the firm of Barristers, Earl & Keith. He never completed his five years as an articled clerk, choosing instead to return to Britain and fight for his country after just one year.

I have no idea what that meant in terms of his qualification to practice, but I do know that he must have got his head down on returning from Russia as he managed to pass his final exams in very short order in June 1921 at which time he was called to the Bar and began to practice on the South Wales Circuit.

Wynne began to establish himself as a Barrister at Law working with Mr Arthur King-Davies of Maesteg. The firm, now known as King Davies & Partners, are still in existence today, operating from Talbot Street in Maesteg.

For some reason Gwladys kept some of Wynne's briefs from early 1922. I imagine they were in his possession because they were the cases he was working on at the time of his death. They relate to local disputes and the detail is fascinating. They also show that by now Wynne had changed his surname to Wynne-Jones. Wynne was his middle name (Llewellyn Wynne Jones) but it was

Llewellyn Wynne Jones c 1919

also the name by which he was known in the family. The story I always knew was that there were so many Jones' in Wales that, in order to stand out and make his name in the legal world, grandfather decided to 'double barrel' his names. I've no idea if he did this formally, but we are all known as Wynne-Jones' now and I feel it is an honour to remember him in this way.

As children, my sister and I used to 'honour' Wynne by dressing up in his wig and gown and playing barristers when staying with grandma.

Just like so many young couples today, Wynne and Gwladys were saving for their own home. At the time of his death, they had taken a house in Merthymawyr Road, Bridgend. They had begun to collect furniture and were planning to move in late summer 1922.

Soldiering was however, clearly in Wynne's heart and in his blood. So it really is no surprise that in July 1920 he raised and took charge of a Territorial Army Unit in Maesteg, The 7th (Cyclist) Battalion, The Welch Regiment and was appointed as a Captain in command of the unit.

TA Commission

Captain L. Wynne Jones, M.C. (Maesteg), Lieut. H. W. J. Powell (Cardiff), and Lieut. C. L. Pendlebury, M.C. (Tongwynlais), who were the officers in charge of the guard of honour inspected by the Prince of Wales on his arrival at Cardiff on Monday evening.—("South Wales News" photo.)

The only information I have about this part of Wynne's life is this rather grainy photo of a newspaper cutting from The South Wales News. Wynne is forming part of the Guard of Honour to the Prince of Wales when he visited Cardiff.

On 12th August 1921 my father, Alfred Philip John Wynne-Jones (known as Philip) came into the world.

Philip was Wynne and Gwladys' first and only child and with the war now well behind them, I have no doubt that they would have felt extremely lucky.

So now the little family was set. Wynne was safely home, his career was taking off, their first child son and heir had arrived, and he was enjoying the Territorial unit he had raised. The future looked bright which, given what they and the whole country had been through must have seemed like a little miracle in itself.

I have only two pictures of Wynne and Philip, but this is about the best.

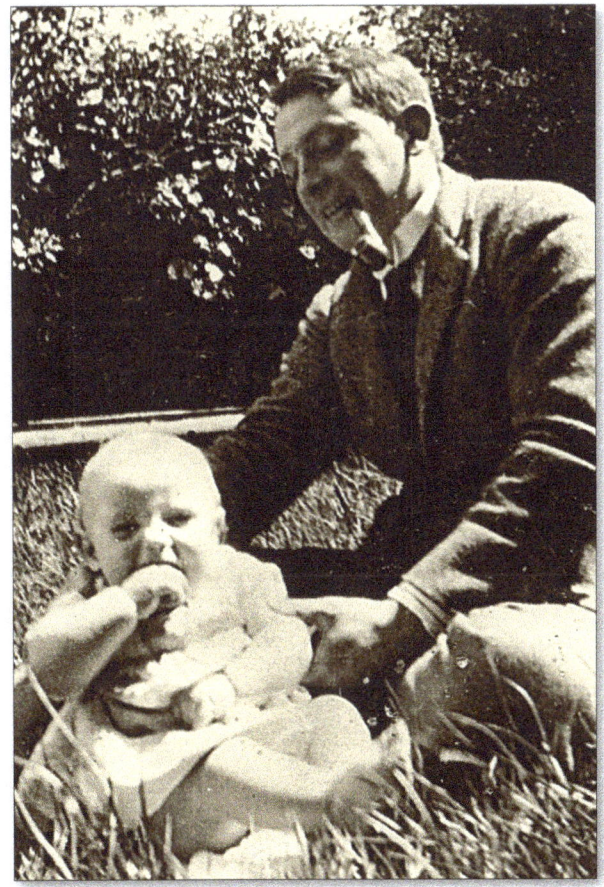

III c. Death

Wynne's death was as random as any seen in war. It was utterly pointless and entirely tragic.

On Sunday 6th August 1922 Wynne was in command of the 7th Battalion, The Welch Regiment, the Territorial Army unit he had raised. They were on duty with a brigade picket in Aberystwyth when the horse he was riding bolted throwing Wynne, after some distance, headfirst into an iron streetlamp where he fell unconscious to the ground. He was taken to hospital and was found to have a fractured skull. Although he did regain consciousness, he died of his injuries four days later on 10th August 1922, two days before his son's first birthday. Gwladys, his sister Annie, his mother Mary and brother in law Gwynn were at his side.

It is impossible to imagine the shock of this tragedy to Gwladys, to Wynne's wider family and to the community in Maesteg. In all the years that I knew her, Gwladys never once spoke to me either of Wynne's life, the tragedy of his death or of his funeral.

Yet the tragedy was keenly felt in the close knit South Wales community. The front page of The Glamorgan Advertiser on Friday 18th August 1922, reported Wynne's death and funeral in some detail.

He was accorded full military honours from the removal of his body from the infirmary to his home, to the funeral day itself. The entire town seems to have turned out to mourn this tragic loss of their own local hero.

When I first came across the reports of his death and funeral, I was very moved. People in Maesteg, like communities all over the country, had endured more death and sadness through the Great War than it is really possible for us to imagine today. Yet here, just four years later, the untimely and tragic loss of one of their own, appears to have affected them all. Perhaps their own losses were still too close to the surface, perhaps the family was well known and loved in the town, perhaps it was simply the shock of someone who may well have been thought of as a local hero; whatever the reason, the town of Maesteg truly honoured my grandfather on that day.

RESEARCHED AND COMPILED BY ALISON CORNELL

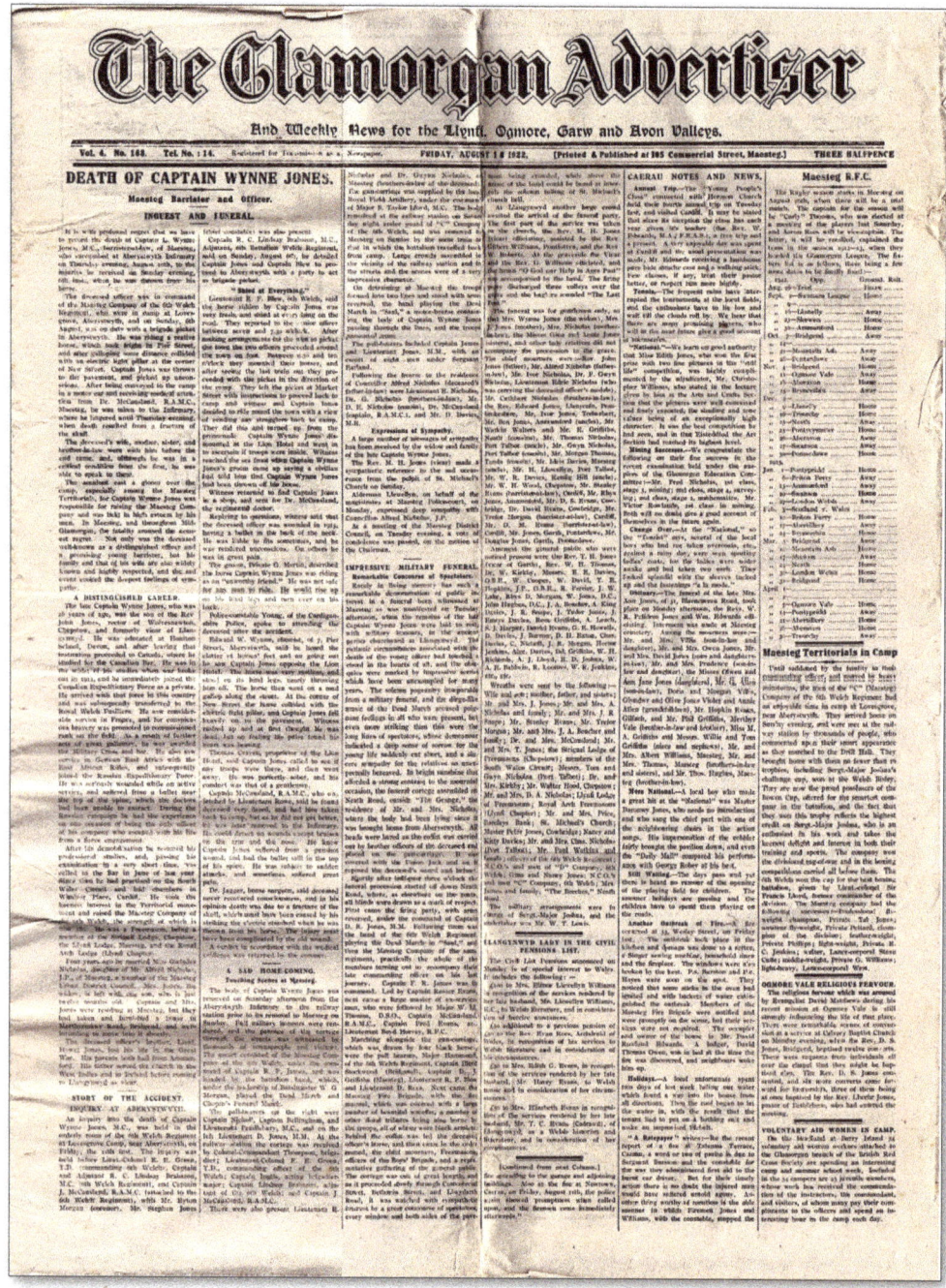

Front page of The Glamorgan Advertiser – Friday August 18 1922. The first four columns are almost entirely given over to a very detailed report of Wynne's funeral.

A full transcript of the newspaper report can be read at Appendix 4

The paper reports;

"Rarely in living memory has such a remarkable demonstration of public interest in a funeral been witnessed in Maesteg, as was manifest on Tuesday afternoon, when the remains of the late Captain Wynne Jones were laid to rest in the ancient parish churchyard at Llangynwyd. "The pathetic circumstances associated with the death of the young officer had touched a chord in the hearts of all, and the obsequies were marked by impressive scenes which have been unexampled for many years. The solemn pageantry inseparable from a military funeral, and the dirge like music of the Dead March aroused poignant feelings in all who were present, but even more striking than this were the long lines of spectators, whose demeanour indicated a deep sense of sorrow for the young life suddenly cut short, and a sincere sympathy for the relatives so unexpectedly bereaved."

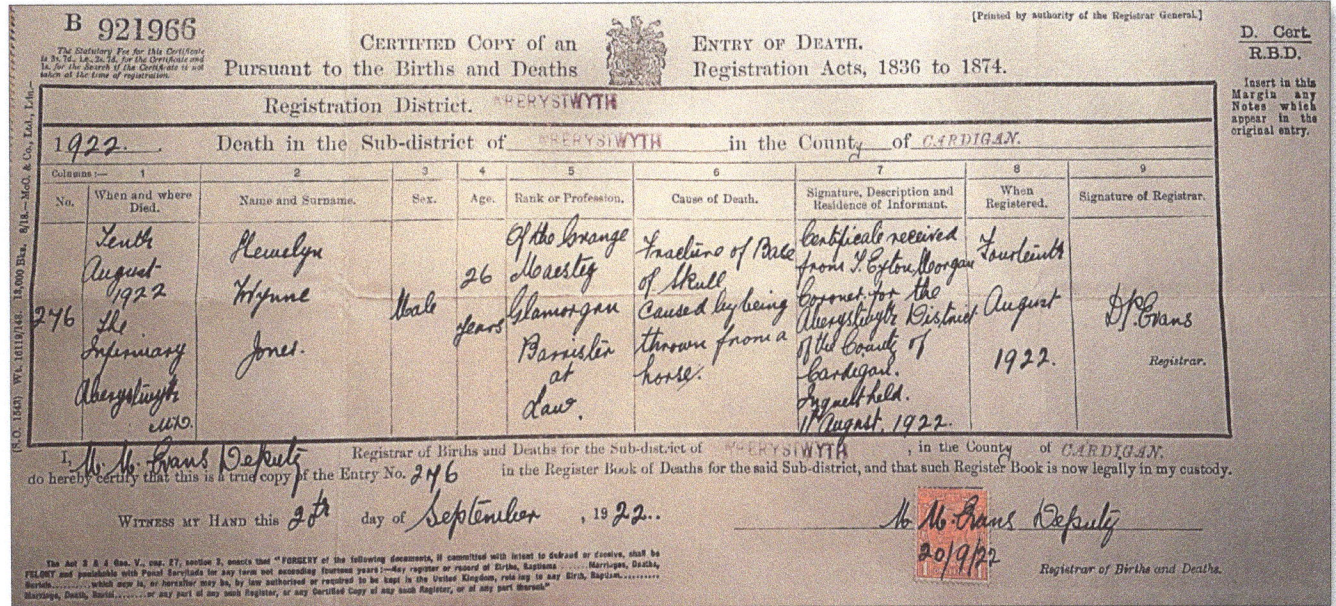

Wynne's death certificate

And so, just as they were starting out, all of Gwladys' hopes and dreams were dashed. The other enormous tragedy of Wynne's untimely death was that my father never really knew his father.

All the furniture they had bought together for their first home, all the plans they had made for their life together ended at a stroke. To this day I use the six mahogany dining chairs they had bought and which my grandmother never disposed of in spite of never having room for them in a home of her own until she was in her 60s. Until I embarked on this project, I had never understood why grandma kept those chairs for so long, but now I understand that they held all her lost dreams.

Yet grandma went on, she lived a full life, she reared a wonderful son, she travelled the world and she did it all with a positivity that I now find utterly humbling.

I found this photo in one of grandma's photo albums. It was a sort of mothers bragging album full of pictures of my father.

In this one he is standing in front of the fence where all their family photos were taken (look back through the book and see), at The Grange on Neath Road.

A little boy wearing his father's hat. Its poignancy is breath taking.

Grandma was a huge part of my life. She often came to visit; she looked after my sister and I when our parents were on holiday and welcomed us to her seaside home in Porthcawl for weeks at a time every summer and in the Easter holidays.

She was great fun and spoilt us rotten – always ordering the Corona man to call when we were with her. She took us regularly to visit Wynne's sister Annie who lived around the corner from her and seemed to generally enjoy spoiling us at every opportunity. Summers always ended with a Knickerbocker Glory at "Fulgoni's Ice Cream Parlour" on the seafront.

Like most of her friends, grandma lived in an almost entirely female society. So many of the young men in her generation having either died in the war or of flu after it. Spinsters and young widows were the norm but that never seemed to make them bitter or stop them having fun. They lived life to the full, perhaps because they truly understood how precious it was.

Grandma travelled all over the world with Wynne's sisters Annie and Gina. They would bring my sister and I exotic traditionally dressed dolls from all the places they visited and entertain us with tails of things seen and done.

I well remember as a child going to Southampton to pick them up from a world cruise. On the way home, while sitting with them in the back of my father's car, grandma started to pull smuggled pearls and jewellery from hidden places in her knickerbockers much to the hilarity and delight of us all. Who would have thought?

I look at their generation, 100 years older than mine and I can only respect them. Their courage in adversity is inspirational and truly worthy of our respect and remembrance.

In his 26 years Wynne achieved more than most of us do in a lifetime or ever would in several.

In the face of such unimaginable loss and heartache Gwladys met the world with a positivity and courage that many struggle to find today without any real experience of loss. She must have had regrets for the life that might have been, but she never let those regrets define her.

My sister Mandy (right) and I with grandma (Gwladys) in our garden in Crawley around 1965.

Dear Grandma and Grandfather

Not until I undertook this project did I really appreciated what incredible people you both were.

I cannot begin to say how much I regret not talking to you more in life grandma. How much I took you for granted and how little I appreciated what your life had been like and how many dreams you never realised.

Only now do I fully grasp all that you achieved grandfather and all that you lost. As strange as it sounds, I had never really considered that had you lived a life of normal length I should have known you well. You would have seen your son grow into a fine man and met your three grandchildren. It's so easy to forget the real price paid by so many young men of your generation. For so long in my mind you have been consigned to the sepia tinted annuls of history and yet we were only a generation apart.

This experience has bought you both to life for me in ways that I had never expected. And what lives.

I am so proud to know that you are my part of my history and so sorry that it has taken me this long to fully understand and appreciate the people you were.

With all my love

Alison
Your grandchild

III d. Additional diary photographs

There are a number of photographs from Wynne's albums for which I have found no obvious place in the diary. Some are labelled some are not, many are of Wynne's fellow officers who may not have been referred to by name in his diary. However, in the interests of completeness I wanted to share them all here so that this book is indeed a comprehensive record of my grandfather's East Africa campaign.

Where a label was written, I include it with the photograph here.

Lt. Clarke
Manchesters & K.A.R.

Lt. Veasey
Leicesters & K.A.R.

RESEARCHED AND COMPILED BY ALISON CORNELL

Capt. Osborne
Scots Greys & 1;5 K.A.R.

Lt. Veasey &
Lt. Clark

Capt. H. Hill
4th K.A.R.

Capt. Griffiths M.C.

Capt. Hon. A. Bailey
E.A.M.R.

Capt. Tait
London Scottish & K.A.R.

Somers, Pat, Jenks, Lamb

McLean   Jenkins the Nigger Master   Simpson taken by Tait

The three pictures have no title, but Wynne is in all three.

My particular apologies for any offense caused by the image title top centre here – it is of its time and I have chosen not to censor.

These pictures were all untitled, but I have been keen to include all the men in the possibly vain hope that someone reading this book might just recognise one of these brave young men from their own family archive.

And finally …..

The last two photographs from Wynne's albums.

Neither one is labelled.

The first is a beautifully detailed photograph of some kind of vessel, I would guess from the lakes. I've no idea if it is one Wynne travelled on but it is quite clearly not a very luxurious looking form of transport!

The last is one of my favourite pictures of all. I'm fairly sure it is of Wynne and he is fishing in a lake with his boy by his side. It is such a rare glimpse of Wynne enjoying some down time which is why I love it so much.

III e. Advertisements from the dairy

At the front and back of grandfather's diary there are a number of pages containing a great deal of information (weights and measures etc…) and also advertisements.

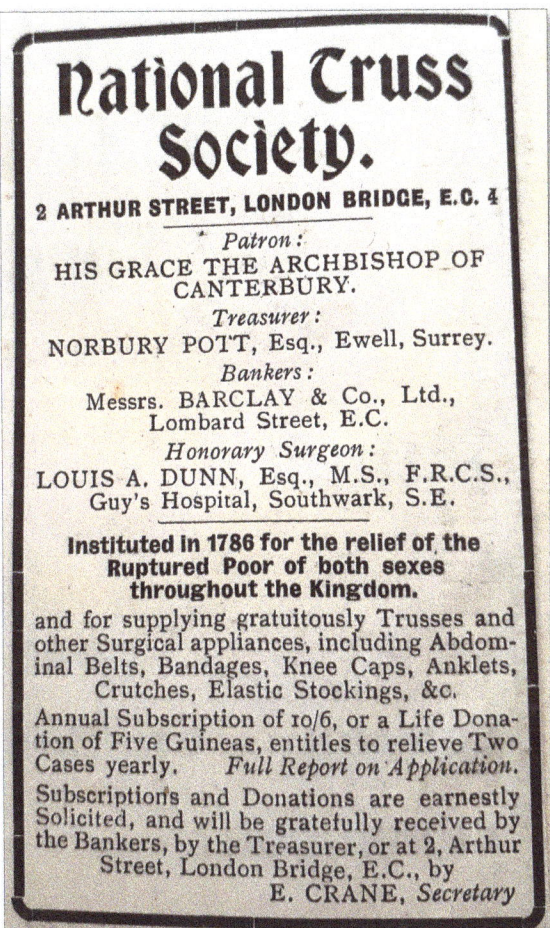

I guess Wynne must have flipped through and read many of them in bored moments in his tent, so I thought it might just be fun to share a few of my favourite bits here.

I begin with a personal favourite – the National Truss Society.

Oh, titter ye not! Clearly this was a real problem for people back in 1918 and remember we are talking pre-NHS.

Men with dreadful hernias, unable to afford either a truss or surgery, would have suffered significant pain and discomfort for years. Indeed, many would have died painfully as a result of untreated hernias.

So although the idea of a truss has become the butt of many a music hall type joke, this charitable offering would have been life transforming for many.

This income and wages table also tells us so much about the income of ordinary working men and women.

When you look at the Truss Society advert asking for 10/6 a year to help two cases, then consider that would be more than a week's wages for many, you begin to understand the scale of the problem.

RESEARCHED AND COMPILED BY ALISON CORNELL

CHARITABLE INSTITUTIONS. 105

Hospital for Consumption and Diseases of the Chest, Brompton.

Patrons: H.M. The King, H.M. The Queen, H.M. Queen Alexandra.
SANATORIUM AND CONVALESCENT HOME, Frimley, Surrey.

In-Patients, 1916 - 1,950   **GREATLY**   Annual Expenditure over £40,000
Out-Patients, 1916 - 7,976   **NEEDS HELP.**   Only Fixed Income under £4,000

The Committee of Management earnestly appeal for new Annual Subscriptions, Donations, and Legacies.   FREDERICK WOOD, Secretary.

THE NATIONAL HOSPITAL
FOR THE PARALYSED & EPILEPTIC,
Queen Square, Bloomsbury, W.C.1.

The oldest and largest voluntary hospital of its kind. There are in the wards seventy soldiers suffering from shattered nerves, blindness, deafness, mutism, and nerve injuries. Subscriptions for maintenance are very earnestly asked for.

THE EARL OF HARROWBY, Treasurer.

I found these adverts/appeals for hospitals really interesting. They are all still in existence today, The Brompton, The National and Evelina.

Thankfully today they are all funded by the NHS.

EVELINA HOSPITAL for Children,
SOUTHWARK, LONDON, S.E.

Under the patronage of their Majesties the King & Queen. Supported entirely by Voluntary Contributions.
Only large Children's Hospital in South London. Situated in its poorest District.

FUNDS GREATLY NEEDED.

Please help this Charity, "not only because it is a Hospital, but because it is a Hospital for Children."

President: Viscount Duncannon, M.P.
Chairman: D. Malcolm Scott, Esq.
Treasurer: Gerald D. Smith, Esq.
Secretary: H. C. Staniland Smith.

It is sobering to consider that all the brave young men coming back from war would have had no automatic free access to healthcare. Many would have had injuries and wounds that would have had lifelong implications, yet they were going to be dependent on charity.

AN INSTITUTION FOR THE PROTECTION OF DOGS AND CATS.
(Or Temporary Home for Lost and Starving Dogs and Cats.) **THE DOGS' HOME** (4, Battersea Park Rd., S.W.8, and Hackbridge, Surrey.)

Patron: His Most Gracious Majesty the King.   President: His Grace The Duke of Portland, K.G.

OBJECTS. 1.—To provide food and shelter for the lost and deserted dogs of London.
2.—To restore lost dogs to their rightful owners.
3.—When good dogs are unclaimed, to find suitable homes for them at nominal charges.
4.—To destroy by a merciful and painless method, all valueless and diseased dogs.

Out-patients' Department, Battersea (Dogs and Cats only), Thursdays, 2.30. Admission by letter, obtainable from Subscribers or Donors. At the Country Branch, Hackbridge, Surrey, Dogs and Cats can be received as boarders, and Dogs for quarantine under the importation of Dogs Order, 1914.

Contributions thankfully received by GUY H. GUILLUM SCOTT, Secretary.

And then of course there was the good old Battersea Dogs Home.

Appendix 1

Hywel Jones – Letters from France
January - March 1917

17 January 1917
38th IBD - B.E.F.

Dear Dada & Mama

I am here temporarily so you better not write till I know my destination. La Belle France is some place, the trains go at a positively violent speed, in fact I've left our port of arrival at 8p.m. & reached here at 4 a.m. this morning. Needless to say, I went to sleep without taking much off beside my boots. I crossed the channel without any casualties & though it snowed all the way & was rather cold I was quite all right. I had some food as we got to port by 1 pm and were told to be at a station 2 mls away before three. It was a rush, but we did it & on our way we passed the statue of the gentle burghers with ropes round their necks in which context I remember doing the above into French prose at school & translating necks by Lez.

On arriving at our station one of our number would insist on falling over the rails as French stations are just bare tracks. As an example of the speed of a French train we found one blocking our way to what we thought was our train. The blocking train was moving at its average rate, so we just jumped on opened a carriage door, walked right through & hopped off the other side.

When we got there, we found it wasn't our train and were told to wait in a place privately run for officers. There we sat after several false alarms till nearly 8 amusing each other by telling yarns of the ghost variety. Then we at last got in, the train always starts off like an express & stops suddenly so everyone was floundering about the carriages. We arrived here quite early in the morning walked up to the camp had some oxo which I made on a Tommie's cooker – a boon & a blessing - & turned in with several moist blankets for company and slept like a top till 8. How long I shall be here I don't know but don't write till you hear from me again.

I expect you'll have received the proofs of my photo. Whatever you do don't have any of me with a grin on my face as they are fiendish in the extreme & not fit for human consumption. I hope you'll like the brooch I sent, it cost very little & it is my xmas present somewhat late.

This is a violently long letter for me, so the air of France must have improved me.

At present, we have a nice sprinkling of snow & a very fair amount of mud. We have quite a decent hut as officer's mess but as always there are innumerable rests & canteens for privates who need all the rest they can get. We are miles behind the lines not even within sound of the guns.

No more news now.

Love to all with love from your loving son.

Hywel

P.T.O.
A photo of a pal should have arrived for me please put it in the drawer with my other photos. That particular chap will be going up to Oxford after the war in fact wherever I go I always get a man who was once head of his own school.

---

21 January 2017
1st Queens - B.E.F.

Dear Dada & Mama

As you can see, I have been posted to a definite Bn & am more or less at the front in other words in Billets behind the lines.

When I get the chance, I am going to send home 2 things one for the pater & one for your museum.

The first is an old book of the last three books of the Aeneid with a French verse translation the date being 1813 1 or 2 years before Waterloo & rather over 100 years old. The other is a leather water bottle as used by the Zouaves or Algerians. Both were picked up by me & not any of these bought souvenirs that are going about but are both rather disreputable as they come from any old town hall which a stray shell had hit rather hard.

I have already given you a pretty full account of my doings from the time I left England to my arrival at the base & so I'll carry on from there.

After spending a day there I marched forth to an old bull-ring where they proposed to put me with some other unfortunates through a form of amusement called a refresher course. After marching some 2 kilos we stopped took off our packs & dumped our rifles & were going to be amused by being thrust headlong into a fiery furnace like Shadrach & Co – called for courtesy a gas chamber – when an orderly came & informed me that the adjutant of the T.B.D. would like to see me. I toddled back & found an invitation to take a draft & myself up the line to join this Bn. Fortunately I had 2 time serving sergeants with me & so I was quite happy. The next day at the hour of 7 having not broken my fast I marched them down to the station, entrained them & by wiles & cunning secured a moderate carriage for myself. We then set off & through the day I lived on biscuits & chocolate.

I got to my destination at 7.30 that evening having travelled at a terrific speed about 15 m.p.h. I spent the night at the rail head 5 officers in a shed about the size of the coal house. In the morning I had breakfast & shortly afterwards moved off to my billets. There I waited for the Bn & settled down.

The part of the line we are in is unpleasant as regards mud only.

No more news now.

Love to all with love from your loving son.

Hywel

P.T.O.
Don't open Wynne's bag till I send the keys.

---

29 January 2017
1st Queens - B.E.F.

Dear Dada & Mama

I think in the last instalment of the history of my life I had finished bringing up a draft.

I stayed in that place from Saturday until Tuesday & moved a little further up. Then the day before yesterday I rose betime in the morning & wandered off up to the front line to prepare for the company. It was a very tiring march up & when I got there, there was plenty to do. As often happens on a dark cold night everyone was a bit cross & I was glad to depart at 19.15 or 12 midnight. Then another long march with another regiment for 4 hrs. I then succeeded in losing my way & went into a hut I found & lay down from 5.30 to 7.30 when it became light & I could find my destination.

I am actually going on a course & for that reason escape the trenches for a short time.

I got to my destination at 9 & had to hop it at 11.45. When I got to the railway, I found that no trains were running so back I came. I had tea at 5 at 6 I was in bed & had breakfast at 10 the next morning so you can imagine I was pretty tired to sleep all that time.

My first experience of the trenches was not thrilling or horrifying but consisted mostly of petrol which tasted of water & unending communication trenches. I expect by now you have received my letters but it's rather early to receive any from you.

No more news now.

Love to all with love from your loving son.

Hywel

31 January 1917
33rd Divisional Infantry School - B.E.F.

Dear Dada & Mama

Here I am & here I shall be for 3 weeks so you can write to me here. I came down in a motor lorry & expect to have a decent time. I spent a whole day in bed in a dug-out on Monday & it was paradise. You must not expect me home as my turn for leave doesn't come till next August & we hope there'll be no need for any then. I am writing this in a little Café which appears to be the warmest place in the village & I always did like warmth when I could get it. What strikes me as humorous is that the work we considered hell with a big H in England we consider Heaven here & of course one must go up the line to realise that a war is on. The shelling & all that is nothing but the miles of trudging through narrow communication trenches is apt to feed one up.

I have now got to the stage where the guns make me think some idiot is slamming the door with most laudable but utterly unnecessary perseverance.

I was told that the people who give their relatives at home the most thrilling accounts of trench life are the A.S.C. men who never see the trenches at all, while I know from censoring letters that is when they are miles away from the trenches that the men say they have shells flying around.

One has to be careful with that sort as they are liable to put down rather more information than is absolutely necessary.

My personal experience is that I had the wind up much more when I saw the flash of the guns for the first time miles away than when I was actually under a slight shell fire. In fact when you are actually under fire you spend all your time speculating as to whether our friend the Bosch has actually seen you or whether he is just slinging his morning anthem. My first instance we had cause to pour our benedictions on the head of a Bosch aeroplane, of a somewhat inquisitive turn of mind.

My bed now has got sheets in it & though it is only 2 weeks it seems years since I slept in a proper bed. The reason I suppose is that I have in the course of 14 days wandered over the face of the earth like the proverbial Jew.

I don't think you can complain that my letters are on the short side in fact I always wonder how I manage to rattle off such a lot of bilge, but I know you prefer that to my customary brevity & laziness of expression.

No more news now. Love to all with love from your loving son.

Hywel

7 February 1917
33rd Divisional Infantry School - B.E.F.

Dear Mama

Thanks very much for your letter, the first sent since I've been in France. I shall be at this place for another fortnight & I'm not sorry either as I'd rather not be in the line until the actual strafe commences.

You needn't worry too much about the cold as it means that there is no mud while this continues but I fancy it'll be thawing very soon. I am sorry to hear that Wynne has been ill again, but it is better that it should happen now than when a serious job is on hand.

At present I'm living in the lap of luxury & actually have a bed with sheets & I can tell you that I sleep like a top from 10 till 7 & on Sundays till about 10. I believe in resting while you can as I know that there are some occasions when circs will not permit of excessive slumber & anyway I always was slightly lazy. I hope the photos have turned up as you say nothing about them in your letter & I am rather anxious concerning them in case you have chosen the ghastly one with a grin on. I told the photographer to send you the proof of that one with the others but that whether you chose it or not they were on no account to supply any, because really it took me some time to nerve myself to get my photo taken & I shall be more than pained if that is to be the result of my meritorious self-denial.

I am at present waiting for an orderly sergeant to come along & inform me that lights are out etc, & when he comes, I go to bed.

I got a Bystander from Annie but could find no letter in it anywhere, so I expect she didn't put one in which is rather a clever solution to come considering the addled state of my brains.

No more news now.

Love to all with love from your loving son.

Hywel

11 February 1917
B.E.F.

Dear Mama

I shall be another 10 days or so here then up the line again for a week or so.

Don't worry about me losing my way & falling on the Bosch I won't go & interview our friend the enemy until the clarion call of duty as the ½ rags call it, make me. I wrote to Wynne at Rouen. I must have been at the base when Wynne said he was only a ¼ of a mile away. It was rather a pity. There was a general hospital there which I passed more than once in the two days I was there. I am sending a cheque to the pater. I have been divorced from my cheque book for some time until I came here. I haven't had half a chance of sending it.

I am having the time of my life here at present & lose no opportunity of staying in bed. I gather from the allusions in the enclosed letter that Annie has been successful in getting her headship. I am very glad to hear it & I have so far condescended as to write & offer my congratulations.

I am glad the photos met with your approval, but you rather left out the most picturesque part of my face when you reject a photo because it displays my ears. Furthermore however much I try to please you invariably assert that I come out better in some rag group than in a serious effort.

The moon seems to have gone west because we never see anything of her now.

Can you let me have Gina's address as I am bothered if I can remember whether it's the 47th or 31st or the other way round or what.

No more news now.

Love to all with love from your loving son.

Hywel

This was the last letter in the collection. Hywel was killed on 4th March 1917.

Sometime later the family received the following letter;

March 14 1917

On the night of Feb 28 1917 the First Battⁿ The Queens RWS Regt went into the front line trenches at a position between Bouchauesnes & Feuillers the first NW of the village of Cleary the second SSE of the same place. On the 4th March 1917 Second Lieut Jones accompanied by his servant were inspecting the men & trenches when passing an ammunition store a shell came over striking a box of small arm ammunitions which exploded immediately killing Private Halladay the officers servant & severely wounded Lieut Jones who I am sorry to say succumbed to his wounds a short time after but he was unconscious.

He was carried to the Medical Officer & was there given every attention but of no avail. We dug his grave & buried him & also his servant in a small cemetery behind the support trenches. All religious ceremonies were executed over the two bodies & also a cross placed over both graves.

This is a true statement as to the death of Second Lieut Jones as I myself witnessed all & if I can be of any use as regards information it will be my duty which I will gladly do to do anything I can.

10343 Private JW Daly
H, Inarter Company
1st Battⁿ The Queens Reg^t
B.E.F.

Hywel's Cap Badge

Appendix 2

Auntie Gina (Jones) - Interviewed by BBC Radio Medway
14 August 1980

Aunty Gina age 98, photographed for her BBC interview

Q. Well Miss Jones, can we go back to the beginning? A very, very long time ago, 96 years. Where abouts were you born?

A. Well I was born in a little welsh village in the Black Mountains in Carmarthenshire near Ammanford. And then I was taken to the West Indies at the age of nine months.

Q. What was your family background? What did your parents do?

A. Well, um, my, my mother was from farming stock and my father from engineering. And then my grandmother had an enormous family. She had nine children, six sons and three daughters. And of those five of the sons, or six of the sons I think were clergymen and one was an architect who migrated to Portland in Oregon where he became one of the senior architects.

Q. The whole of your background really is Wales I suppose and with a name like Jones that's hardly really surprising.

A. Well we're all Welsh. Now the family has begun to spread itself and they're extremely mongrel, the lot of them. But until now we were pure bred Welsh.

Q. You mentioned your father and you said you went to the West Indies when you were nine months old, what did your father do at this time?

A. Well he went out really as a school master in one of the colleges out in St Kitts in Nevis. And then we followed on, my mother and myself, we followed on when I was nine months old and later, he became ordained by the Bishop of Antigua and he was there for quite a number of years. He had, he was chaplain to the Bishop of Antigua at one time and he had a very strenuous life for he had three churches, five schools, for then they were responsible for the schools, and also, he undertook to try and educate his own children at which he wasn't terribly good because he always thought we were mentally deficient.

Q. How many were there in the family, as well as yourself?

A. Well as a matter of fact we were um six children but four died in very early youth. Well in childhood really. And then he also undertook to, um, he was rather sorry for the planters' sons who had nobody to educate them as of course no white child would go to school with coloured people. It wasn't really a snobbery; it was just done after the…. you see it wasn't very long after slavery was abolished (1833) that we came into existence there because it was 1865, so all our servants were the children of slaves and we were taught by the servants the history of slavery. They told us a great deal about slavery and also what they felt when they were liberated. How lost they were, how they were longing for some instruction as how to manage their own lives.

Q. How long were you out in the West Indies for?

A. We had a little break and my father brought us over and we came err Cloteran[1] in Ireland. Church of Ireland Parson in a comic little village in Galway. It was very, very primitive I have an idea that I remember that they had chickens running into their houses and roosting on the bedposts. Altogether it was an extremely primitive thing. I was about seven then and as far as I can remember we were there for about two years when he returned to the West Indies and I got very little education actually. I think about two hours a day at the most and I came over when I was fourteen and found life rather difficult for the um, there's a tremendous difference between life in the West Indies and life in a little Welsh colliery district.

Q. Can we go back just a minute to the West Indies? What were the conditions like there? You mentioned it was what, twenty years after the end of slavery, but what were the conditions like generally for white settlers?

A. Oh they, it was really very good. Far superior to England and of course I think we got a little bit of the aristocratic touch about us. Because I remember when I came to England and we could only afford a very young little maid and she addressed me by my Christian name which I objected to strongly because she didn't put 'Miss' in front of it. Well I was completely cured, my snobbery has been cured by that young girl, when she just put her head back and shouted with laughter till it reverberated all over the mountains – so I was put in my place by that little welsh girl.

Q. So this was fourteen when you, you were fourteen when you came back from the West Indies finally

A. Finally well yes. Anyhow, it was when Gladstone was buried (1898)

Q. You can actually remember that particular incident, can you? Gladstone's funeral.

A. Oooh yes. I didn't see the funeral, but it was the papers, newspapers that I didn't know much about. It was all about newspapers these…, I couldn't think why there was all this commotion in the newspapers and why the boys were running about proclaiming it on platform and that sort of thing it was altogether and then I remember the incident of the first time I went into a lift. We went in what I thought was a little box, but I had no idea it was going to move.

---

[1] Can't find this place in County Galway, so not sure I have heard it right, but please let me know if you can solve the mystery!

Q. Where was this, in London?

A. This was in London, yes.

Q. So what did you do when you actually came back from the West Indies? You presumably continued your education in Britain.

A. Well for a short time, oh, not many months, they were hunting for a school for me and I.. in a little village, I went to the village school for about six months and finally I went to a boarding school in Clifton in Bristol and I was there until I was nineteen.

Q. What we would call these days perhaps a finishing school where you study the finer points of life?

A. No I wouldn't call it a finishing school it was just a girl's public school and it was a very good school.

Q. This was around the turn of the century I suppose. About the time Queen Victoria died.

A. it was about the time when I was at school when Queen Victoria visited Bristol and it was a great event in our lives then and I expected to see her sitting in all her regalia with her crown on her head and I was absolutely horror struck when there was this little woman in black, tiny little woman in black with a black parasol. I wept.

Q. You were disappointed?

A. I certainly was disappointed. (laughs)

Q. What else do you remember of that particular occasion?

A. Well I can't remember my school days very well, I think it was a struggle for me in school because, not having had proper education until I was fourteen, I had a struggle to keep pace. But fortunately I usually managed to be about second in the form, and I took the higher certificate, you know, but I was so bad at French that had I failed in French, I would not have got my Oxford and Cambridge higher certificate. I couldn't have got it and I had to be grateful to my French teacher who was welsh and took an interest in me for that reason and coached me and I actually got through in French, so I got my certificate.

Q. What were your best subjects in school though?

A. Mathematics.

Q. And had you at this time any idea what you wanted to do when you left school? Because those days presumably young ladies didn't go out to work did they?

A. Well, at the age of seven I knew exactly what I was going to be. I said I was going to be a nurse and I never wavered one minute from it. And as a child I remember perfectly being taken out by a little black maid on to a beach where there was a lazaretto[2] and this was cordoned off with wire netting and I remember I must have been three. Remember crawling under it and playing with the lepers and when I got to understand about leprosy and I felt that I might get it and it was a great nightmare to me, this thought of being a leper. But I decided I'd be a nurse in a leper colony.

Q. This was a common disease presumably in the West Indies at the time?

A. Ooh yes. They were wandering about and err we had a, my father and mother had a very difficult life there. They were quite happy, but they had a very difficult life and they used to have Christmas dinner for the poor people you know, and I remember one man with double dislocation of hip and he frightened me to death. He was like a sort of frog hopping along. You see there was nothing that could be done for him and I was terrified of him and my mother would insist on my taking his old calabash with his food in it to him. That's going back a bit now.

Q. That really got you over any kind of worries or fears you might have of illness or physical disability I suppose.

A. I suppose it did but why I decided I was going to be a nurse at seven I'll never know, and I started training at a 1906.

Q. And where did you train?

A. I've been in sixteen hospitals.

Q. You didn't train in all sixteen, did you?

A. Well, I did special training in several. I did training in um, special eye training. I did massage and electrical work. I did maternity and of course general training in Winchester; my general training was in Winchester.

Q. So when did your training end?

A. Well I went to America, to Hollywood in 1913.

Q. Any particular reason why you went to Hollywood?

A. A friend of mine decided that we were so badly paid, and I had so many certificates that she felt I would do much better out in America.

Q. And did you?

A. I did extremely well in America. I found the hospitals there magnificent. I was in charge of an orthopaedic department in Hollywood in the children's hospital. A very magnificent hospital in

---

[2] A *lazaretto* or lazaret is a quarantine station for maritime travellers. Lazarets can be ships permanently at anchor, isolated islands, or mainland buildings.

Hollywood. Then of course, war was declared, and I felt I had to come back which I did. And I joined Queen Alexandra's imperial nursing service and I landed in Plymouth and that was quite an experience. For so many of the people came from all over the world, the patients were from all over the world and the poor Negros came and got measles and died so all their patriotisms it seemed very tragic. So after that, after about nine months in Plymouth I went to Salonica and we arrived in Salonica and it was then we discovered we were going to nurse the Serbs and not the English which was, to us, a shock. We didn't know what to expect.

Q. Serbia being what is part of Yugoslavia these days.

A. it is, it was yes. Oh the Slovines, I think they all joined up later. But at the moment they were Serbs when we were out there. And when we arrived in Salonika nothing was ready for us. The hospital was way up the country and we were taken back to Malta where we stayed for a few weeks until once more we landed in Salonika and at dead of night we got into these rather rugged old trains and were driven all night until we arrived up in a little valley called Verticop was the name of the place and there were two hospitals, one was territorial and the other was Queen Alexanders. And there were no patients for some time then the dead of night they came in in paniers on the side of mules and we were really horrified. My medical officer was a Captain Monserrat who I think was the father of the author and he was a delightful man he really was and my ward was the first, my tent was the first to be opened up and there we were wrestling with these huge men and I was all for getting them settled and undressed and settled until one nurse came and told me don't you think you better let them sleep which I being the boss at the time sounded I was a little mentally deficient. However we started the next morning and it was terribly funny not knowing the language at least we'd learnt two or three sentences, but we invariably used the wrong sentence. There'd be two sentences that we knew, one was *"carcus terraneum"* and the other was *"cads terraneum"*. Now I never knew which was which but when I said one of them they began counting on their fingers but I wanted them to tell me where they were wounded but I was asking them when were they wounded but however, we got over that difficulty by saying *"dobro"* and *"nay dobro"* good and not good and that's how we managed to converse.

Q. Now where else did you see service during the First World War then?

A. Well I saw, I was always with the Serbs but after a while I was very worried I had, was removed down to nearer the front, err nearer Salonika. I wasn't a bit happy there and there we got all of us, nearly all of us got malaria. I know one night I was going off duty and I felt extremely funny, not ill but odd. And I took my temperature and it was 106! I took the other nurses' temperature and she was 102. So as I was the boss I thought I ought to stay on because she was 102, but then I realised that I would have to be carried off and the time of the night nurses to come on was approaching so I went across the camp and got hold of the home sister and when she took my temperature she raced down to the medical officers who were having their dinner and they came up and I remember his flashing a light in my face and saying *"Sister you've been crying"* and I was furious I hadn't been crying but I suppose my temperature was so high that my eyes were red and we had a lot of recurrent malaria there.

Q. Did you stay in the Serbian area for the whole of the war?

A. No, oh no. I then moved to another hospital up in a place called Sorovich that was around the Albanian border and we really had quite a happy time there. We had the Russians corralled at the bottom of the mountain. And all night, that was when you know 1917 and they used to sing most beautifully, and I must say that was a very nice part of the job. We had terrible, terrible winters shocking and we were under canvass the whole time. Well when I returned to England.

Q. That was after the war?

A. 1918. I was stationed in Rippon and there it was a frightfully sad experience. For so many of the men who had escaped the war had come back, they were sent up, they contracted this horrible Spanish flu and they came up to Rippon and in no time at all they nearly all went down with this flu. And so many of these great big strong men died. And many, many had lost their memories, and many had lost their speech, the reaction was terrible. I remember one night I was doing my rounds and I passed the bed where I'd never heard a sound before and all of a sudden there was this voice. The man had recovered his voice in the middle of the night and the man was waving his hands about, he was so terrified he was going to lose it again.

And finally I left there because they thought I had a patch of TB and I was forced to live out of doors. And then I became a Health Visitor in Swansea and there I was for quite a number of years and I got rather restless and then I saw an advert for a superintendent of Health Visitors in Nassau, and I went off to Nassau and I was there for six years.

Q. In the Bahamas?

A. In the Bahamas.

Aunty Gina in the Bahamas

Q. How did you come to Sheerness?

A. Now I am very attached to Sheerness. I am much happier in Sheerness than I was in the Bahamas. Of course I was very interested in the Bahamas because you met such exciting people like travellers and explorers and big professors. Altogether you met such interesting people in the Bahamas but what happened was, there was no pension scheme when I left England and it was very difficult for me after six years of not being contributing to pensions to be taken on. Well Sheerness was kind to me and took me on and here I've been very happy for forty years.

Q. So you were here for the duration of the last war?

A. I was here. Every time I come back to England there's a war or at least there've been two wars when I've returned to England. And I must say that I've found Sheppey people the kindest and really most helpful people. I've never had a minute's trouble.

Q. Have you ever had any regrets in your chosen career, you've been nursing for all those years, what, seventy years now?

A. Never, never. Yes, yes, it is isn't it? I was 67 when the council got rid of me because they kept me on two extra years. And then I went in and I worked till I was 82 in homes for mother and babies and I found that most interesting. And then I also went into a home for probation, well that was a most awful experience. I never knew that such children existed. It was an eye opener.

Q. Now it seems after a very, very long life and a busy life that you must get rather bored with yourself these days. What do you do with your time now?

A. Well actually I don't get bored. I seem to have plenty of work to do. As I say, I worked till I was 82 so I haven't had such a long retirement have I (laughs)

Q. Is there anything that you haven't done in your life that you would still like to do? Anything you would like to see?

A. No quite frankly I've had a very happy, most exciting life. I don't think I have any regrets there may be one perhaps

Q. What's that?

A. Oh, well I'm not telling you! (laughs)

Q. Finally I must ask the question which I think everybody is tempted to ask you; what do you attribute your long life to?

A. Heredity I should say. There have been some very long lived people in my family but I, I'm outdoing them all. I am the oldest of the clan and now I look for respect from those below me (laughs)

Q. You certainly get it from us, and I'll come back, and I'll see you when you're 100

A. (Laughs) No, I haven't any great desire to be 100. No great desire.

Q. Well Miss Jones, thank you very much indeed for personally speaking. It's been most interesting.

Appendix 3

A Poem found amongst my Auntie Annie's effects.

<u>A Summers Day's Reverie by the Sea</u>

Far away across the ocean in the Islands of the west
Where, arrayed in tropic splendour beauteous nature's at her best:
Where the great mysterious Gulf Stream flowing eastwards has its source,
There, on beauteous little Nevis, thy sweet life began its course.

In a sea of glowing sapphire those West Indian Islands lie –
Emerald Isles of deep green lustre, canopied by a deep blue sky,
And bejewelled dreamy Nevis, with it's fascinating charms
With its feathery leaved acacias, cactus trees and graceful palms.

Vies with the best of heavens beauty, 'tis Earths loveliest paradise
And 'twas in that western Eden you first opened your blue eyes!
How I envy you your childhood spent mid such delightful scenes,
Playing on that sunny seashore – racing over flowery greens!

Sometimes wandering in the brushwood, where prolific orchids grow,
Gleaming through the dense dark herbage with a bright and vivid glow.
Often rambling through plantations, or by low thatched negro's huts
Softly shaded by tall palm trees, treading 'neath their loads of nuts.

RESEARCHED AND COMPILED BY ALISON CORNELL

Sometimes watching Picanninnies vigorously engaged in play,
And, there too, are buxom negresses bounded with bandanas gay.
While the negroes who oft pass you with their easy careless gaits,
Wear cool leaves of shady wideness stuck upon their woolly packs.

Ah! when visions of your childhood rise before your eyes betimes,
Yearning thoughts must needs possess you to be back in those soft climes.
And those thoughts I can imagine, shape themselves in words like this –
"Oh! to see once more my birthplace, home of beauty, Isle of bliss.

Oh! to view once more the glories so profusely lavished there.
Oh! to breath once more the odours of that cinnamon-scented air.
I shall never, never, never like this dreary Ogmore Vale
With its north winds coal dust laden, and its meadows strewn with shade.

For my heart is in that Island, mid the scenes I loved to roam,
Playing on its golden fringes in the sea waves' silvery foam."
With these plaints you let your fancy stirred by such reminiscences
Have full sway till its exhausted, and on reason once more leans.

By and by will come a lover, (who or whom, I do not know)
Who will fill your eyes with lovelight and your heart with love's warm glow.
In that light you'll see this valley in such hues that it shall be
Dearer to you and even lovelier than that Eden o'er the sea.

W.P. - *The Cliffs, Llantwit Major*

Appendix 4

The Glamorgan Advertiser

Friday August 18 1922

DEATH OF CAPTAIN WYNNE JONES

Maesteg Barrister and Officer

INQUEST AND FUNERAL

It is with profound regret that we have to record the death of Captain L. Wynne Jones, M.C., barrister-at-law, of Maesteg, who succumbed at Aberystwyth Infirmary on Thursday evening, August 10th, to the injuries he received on Sunday evening, 6th inst., when he was thrown from his horse.

The deceased officer was in command of the Maesteg Company of the 6th Welch Regiment, who were in camp at Lovesgrove, Aberystwyth, and on Sunday, 6th August, was on duty with a brigade picket in Aberystwyth. He was riding a restive horse, which took fright in Pier Street, and after galloping some distance collided with an electric light pillar at the corner of New Street. Captain Jones was thrown to the pavement and picked up unconscious. After being conveyed to the camp in a motor car and receiving medical attention from Dr. Mc Causland, R.A.M.C., Maesteg, he was taken to the Infirmary, where he lingered until Thursday evening, when death resulted from a fracture of the skull.

The deceased's wife, mother, sister and brother-in-law were with him before the end came, and, although he was in a critical condition from the first, he was able to speak to them.

The accident cast a gloom over the camp, especially among the Maesteg Territorials, for Captain Wynne Jones was responsible for raising the Maesteg Company and was held in high esteem by his men. In Maesteg, and throughout Mid-Glamorgan, the fatality aroused the keenest regret. Not only was the deceased well-known as a distinguished officer and a promising young barrister, but his family and that of his wife are also widely known and highly respected, and the sad event evoked the deepest feelings of sympathy.

A DISTINGUISHED CAREER

The late Captain Wynne Jones, who was 26 years of age, was the son of the Rev John Jones, rector of Wolvesnewton, Chepstow, and formerly vicar of Llangynwyd. He was educated at Honiton School, Devon, and after leaving that institution proceeded to Canada, where he studied for the Canadian Bar. He was in the midst of his studies when war broke out in 1914, and he immediately joined the Canadian Expeditionary Force as a private. He arrived with that force in this country and was subsequently transferred to the Royal Welch Fusiliers. He saw considerable service in France, and for conspicuous bravery was promoted to commissioned rank on the field. As a result of further acts of great gallantry, he was awarded the Military Cross and bar. He also saw service in German East Africa with the East African Rifles, and subsequently joined the Russian Expeditionary Force. He was seriously wounded while on active service and suffered from a bullet near the top of his spine, which the doctors had been unable to extract. During the Russian campaign he had the experience on one occasion of being the only officer of his company who escaped with his life from a fierce engagement.

After his demobilisation he resumed his professional studies, and, passing his examination in a very short time, was called to the bar in June of last year. Since then he had practiced on the South wales Circuit and had chambers in Windsor Place, Cardiff. He took the keenest interest in the Territorial movement and raised the Maesteg Company of the 6th Welch, the strength of which is now 180. He was a Freemason, being a member of the Striguil Lodge, Chepstow, the Llynfi Lodge, Maesteg, and the Royal Arch Lodge (Llynfi Chapter).

Four years ago he married Miss Gwladys Nicholas, daughter of Mr Alfred Nicholas, J.P., of Maesteg, a member of the Maesteg Urban District Council. Mrs. Jones, the widow, is left with one son, who is just twelve months old. Captain and Mrs. Jones were residing at Maesteg, but they had taken and furnished a house in Merthyrmawr Road, Bridgend, and were intending to move into it shortly.

The deceased officer's brother, Lieut. Hywel Jones, lost his life in the Great War. His parents both hail from Ammanford. His father served the church in the West Indies and in Ireland before coming to Llangynwyd as vicar.

STORY OF THE ACCIDENT.
INQUIRY AT ABERYSTWYTH.

An inquiry into the death of Captain Wynne Jones, M.C., was held in the orderly room of the 6th Welch Regiment at Lovesgrove camp, near Aberystwyth, on Friday, the 11th inst. The inquiry was held before Lieut.-Colonel E.E. Green, T.D. (commanding 6th Welch)), Captain and Adjutant R.C. Lindsay Brabazon, M.C. (6th Welch Regiment), and Captain J. McCausland, R.A.M.C. (attached to the 6th Welch Regiment), with Mr. Eyton Morgan (coroner). Mr. Stephen Jones (chief constable) was also present.

Captain R.C. Lindsay Brabazon, M.C., Adjutant, 6th Battalion Welch Regiment, said on Sunday, august 6th, he detailed Captain Jones and Captain Blew to proceed to Aberystwyth with a party to act as brigade picket.

Lieutenant R.F. Blew, 6th Welch, said the horse ridden by Captain Jones was very fresh, and shied at everything on the road. They reported to the senior officer between seven and 7.30 o'clock. After making arrangements for the men to picket the town the two officers proceeded around the town on foot. Between 9.30 and ten o'clock they mounted their horses, and after seeing the last train out they proceeded with the picket in the direction of the camp. They left the picket at Market Street with instructions to proceed back to camp and witness and Captain Jones decided to ride around the town with a view of sending any stragglers back to camp. They did this and turned up from the promenade. Captain Wynne Jones dismounted at The Lion Hotel and went in to ascertain if troops were inside. Witness reached the sea front when Captain Wynne Jones's groom came up saying a civilian had told him that Captain Wynne Jones had been thrown off his horse.

Witness returned to find Captain Jones in a shop, and sent for Dr. McCausland, the regimental doctor.

Replying to questions, witness said that the deceased officer was wounded in 1915, having a bullet in the back of the neck. He was liable to fits sometimes, and he was rendered unconscious. On others he was in great pain.

The groom, Private G. Martin, described the horse Captain Wynne Jones was riding as an "unworthy friend." He was not safe for any man to ride. He would rise up on his hind legs and turn over on his back.

Police constable Young, of the Cardiganshire Police, spoke to attending the deceased after the accident.

Edward W. Wynne, chemist, of 7, Pier Street, Aberystwyth, said he heard the clatter of horses' feet and on-going out he saw Captain Jones opposite the Lion Hotel. The horse was very restless, and stood on its hind legs, nearly throwing him off. The horse then went on a mad gallop along the street. At the corner of New Street the horse collided with the electric light pillar, and Captain Jones fell heavily on to the pavement. Witness rushed up and at first thought he was dead, but on feeling his pulse found his heart was beating.

Thomas Craven, proprietor of the Lion Hotel, said Captain Jones called to see if any troops were there, and then went away. He was perfectly sober, and his conduct was that of a gentleman.

Captain McCausland, R.A.M.C., who was fetched by Lieutenant Rowe, said he found (the) deceased very dazed, and had him taken back to camp, but as he did not get better, he was later removed to the Infirmary. He could detect no wounds except bruises on the arm and nose. He knew Captain Jones suffered from a gunshot wound and had the bullet still in the top of his spine. He was subject to sudden attacks, and sometimes suffered great pain.

Dt. Jagger, house surgeon, said deceased never recovered consciousness, and in his opinion, death was due to a fracture of the skull, which must have been caused by his striking the electric standard when he was thrown from his horse. The injury must have been complicated by his old wound.

A verdict in accordance with the medical evidence was returned by the coroner.

A SAD HOMECOMING.
Touching Scenes at Maesteg.
The body of Captain Wynne Jones was removed on Saturday afternoon from the Aberystwyth Infirmary to the railway station prior to its removal to Maesteg on Sunday. Full military honours were rendered, and the passage of the cortege through the streets was witnessed by thousands of townspeople and visitors. The escort consisted of the Maesteg Company of the 6th Welch, under the command of Captain R.F. James, and was headed by the battalion band, which under the leadership of Bandmaster W.G. Morgan, played the Dead march and Chopin's Funeral March.

The pall-bearers on the right were Captain Nickoll, Captain Bellingham, and Lieutenant Pendlebury, M.C., and on the left Lieutenant D. Jones, M.M. At the railway station the cortege was received by Colonel-Commandant Thompson, brigadier; lieutenant-Colonel E.E. Green, T.D., commanding officer of the 6th Welch; Captain Inglis, acting brigadier-major; Captain Lindsay Brabazon, adjutant of the 6th Welch; and Captain J. McCausland, R.A.M.C.

There were also present Lieutenant E. Nicholas and Dr. Gwynn Nicholas, of Maesteg (brother-in-law of the deceased). The gun-carriage was supplied by the local Royal Field Artillery, under the command of Major B. Taylor Lloyd, M.C. The body remained at the railway station on Saturday night under guard of "C" Company of the 6th Welch and was removed to Maesteg on Sunday by the same train as that in which the battalion travelled back from camp. Large crowds assembled in the vicinity of the railway station and in the streets and the scenes were of a very impressive character.

On detraining at Maesteg the troops formed into two lines and stood with arms reversed, the band playing the Dead March in "Saul," a motor-hearse containing the body of Captain Wynne Jones passing through lines, and the troops presented arms.

The pall-bearers included Captain James and Lieutenant Jones, M.M., with an escort of eight men under Sergeant Earland.

Following the hearse to the residence of Councillor Alfred Nicholas (deceased's father-in-law) were Lieutenant E. Nicholas, Dr. G. Nicholas (brothers-in-law), Mr D.E. Nicholas (cousin), Dr. McCausland (captain, R.A.M.C.), and Mr D. Davies M.E.

Expressions of Sympathy.
A large number of messages of sympathy has been received by the widow and family of the late Captain Wynne Jones.

The Rev. M.H. Jones (vicar) made a sympathetic reference to the sad occurrence from the pulpit of St. Michael's Church on Sunday.

Alderman Llewellyn, on behalf of the magistrates at Maesteg Police-court, on Monday, expressed deep sympathy with Councillor Alfred Nicholas, J.P.

At a meeting of the Maesteg District Council, on Tuesday evening, a vote of condolence was passed, on the motion of the Chairman.

IMPRESSIVE MILITARY FUNERAL.
Remarkable Concourse of Spectators.
Rarely in living memory has such a remarkable demonstration of public interest in a funeral been witnessed in Maesteg, as was manifest on Tuesday afternoon, when the remains of the late Captain Wynne Jones were laid to rest in the ancient parish churchyard at Llangynwyd.

The pathetic circumstances associated with the death of the young officer had touched a chord in the hearts of all, and the obsequies were marked by impressive scenes which have been unexampled for many years. The solemn pageantry inseparable from a military funeral, and the dirge-like music of the Dead March aroused poignant feelings in all who were present, but even more striking than this were the long lines of spectators, whose demeanour indicated a deep sense of sorrow for the young life suddenly cut short, and a sincere sympathy for the relatives so unexpectedly bereaved. In bright sunshine that afforded a strong contrast to the mournful occasion, the funeral cortege assembled on Neath Road, outside "The Grange" the residence of Mr. and Mrs. Nicholas, where the body had been lying since it was brought home from Aberystwyth. All heads were bared as the coffin was carried out by brother officers of the deceased and placed on the gun-carriage. It was covered with the Union Jack and on it reposed the deceased's sword and helmet.

Shortly after half past three o'clock the funeral procession started off down Neath Road, where, as elsewhere on the route, all blinds were drawn as a mark of respect. First came the firing party, with arms reversed, under the command of Captain D.R. Jones, M.M. Following them was the band of the 6th Welch regiment, playing the Dead March in "Saul," and then the Maesteg Company of the same regiment, practically the whole of the members turning out to accompany their late commanding officer on his last journey. Captain F.R. James was in command. Led by Captain Rosser Evans, next came a large muster of ex-servicemen, who were followed by Major W. Ll. Thomas, D.S.O., Captain McCausland, R.A.M.C., Captain Fred Evans, and Lieutenant Boyd Harvey, R.F.C.

Marching alongside the gun-carriage, which was drawn by four black horses, were the pall bearers, Major Hammond, of the 6th Welch Regiment, Captain D.J. Griffiths (Maesteg), Lieutenant R.F. Blow and Lieutenant D. Rees. Next came the Maesteg Fire Brigade, with the fire manual, which was covered with a large number of beautiful wreaths, a number of other floral tributes being also bourn by the troops, all of whom wore black armlets. Behind the coffin was led the deceased officer's horse, and then came in order named, the chief mourners, Freemasons, officers of the Boys' Brigade, and a representative gathering of the general public.

The cortege was one of great length, and as it proceeded slowly through Commercial Street, Bethania Street, and Llwydarth Road, it was watched with sympathetic interest by a great concourse of spectators, every window and both sides of the pavement being crowded, while above the music of the band could be heard at intervals the solemn tolling of St. Michael's church bell.

At Llangynwyd another large crowd awaited the arrival of the funeral party. The first part of the service was taken in the church, the Rev. M.H. Jones (vicar) officiating, assisted by the Rev. Gilbert Williams, Pontlottyn, and the Rev. W. Roberts. At the graveside the vicar and the Rev. G. Williams officiated, and the hymn "O God our Help in Ages Past" was accompanied by the band. The firing party discharged three volleys over the grave and the buglers sounded "The Last Post."

The funeral was for gentlemen only, so that Mrs. Wynne Jones (the widow), Mrs J. Jones (mother), Mrs. Nicholas (mother-in-law), the Misses Gina and Annie Jones (sisters), and other lady relatives did not accompany the procession to the grave.

The chief mourners were: Rev. John Jones (father), Mr Alfred Nicholas (father-in-law), Mr Ivor Nicholas, Dr. F. Gwyn Nicholas, Lieutenant Edric Nicholas (who was carrying the deceased officer's medals), Mr. Cuthbert Nicholas (brothers-in-law), the Rev. Edward Jones, Llanycefn, Pembrokeshire, Mr. Ivor Jones, Treherbert, Mr Ben Jones, Ammanford (uncles), Mr. Watkin Walters and Mr. E Griffiths, Neath (cousins), Mr. Thomas Nicholas, Port Talbot (uncle), Mr. Gwyn Nicholas, Port Talbot (cousin), Mr Morgan Thomas, Tondu (cousin), Mr. Idris Davies, Maesteg (uncle), Mr. H. Llewellyn, Port Talbot, Mr. W.R. Davies, Kenfig Hill (uncle), Mr W.H. Wood, Chepstow, Mr. Stanley Evans (barrister-at-law), Cardiff, Mr. D.M. Evans (barrister-at-law) Cardiff, Mr. Jones, Garth, Pontardawe, Mr. Douglas Jones, Garth, Pontardawe.

Amongst the general public who were notices present were the Rev. T.H. Jones (vicar of Garth), Rev. W.H. Thomas, Dr. W. Kirby, Messers. E.E. Davies, O.B.E., W. Cooper, W. David, T.E. Hopkins, J.P., O.B.E., R. Ferrier, J.W. Lake, Rhys D. Morgan, W. Jones, D.C., John Hughes, D.C., J.A. Boucher, A. King Davies, J.R. Snape, J. Tudor Jones, J Emrys Davies, Rees Griffiths, A Leach, S.J. Harpur, Daniel Evans, G.E. Howells, D. Davies, J. Barrow, D.H. Exton, Chas. Davies, C. Nicholl, J.R. Morgan, Hector Jenkins, Alec. Davies, Dd. Griffiths, W.H. Richards, A.J. Lloyd, E.D. Joshua, W.A.E. Baldwin, R. Loomes, W.R. Jenkins, etc., etc.

Wreaths were sent by the following: -
Wife and son; mother, father, and sisters; Mr. and Mrs. J. Jones; Mr. and Mrs. A. Nicholas and family; Mr. and Mrs. J.R. Snape; Mr. Stanley Evans; Mr. Trefor Morgan;

Mr. and Mrs. J.A. Boucher and family; Dr. and Mrs. McCausland; Mr. and Mrs. T. Jones; the Strigual Lodge of Freemasons (Chepstow); members of the South wales Circuit; Messers. Tom and Gwyn Nicholas (Port Talbot); Dr. and Mrs. Kirkby; Mr. Walter Hood, Chepstow; Mr. and Mrs. D.A. Nicholas; Llynfi Lodge of Freemasons; Royal Arch Freemasons (Llynfi Chapter); Mr. and Mrs. Price, Barclays Bank; St. Michael's Church; Master Peter Jones, Cowbridge; Nancy and Kitty Davies; Mr. and Mrs. Chas. Nicholas (Port Talbot); Mr. Paul Watkins and family; officers of the 6th Welch Regiment; N.C.O.'s and men of "D" Company, 6th Welch; Gina and Nancy Jones; N.C.O.'s and men "C" Company, 6th Welch; Mrs. James and family, "The Beeches," Neath Road.

The military arrangements were in charge of Sergt. Major Joshua, and the undertaker was Mr. W.T. Lewis.

References

1. Tip & Run by Edward Paice, published by Orion Publishing Co ISBN: 9780753823491

2. https://en.wikipedia.org/wiki/SMS_K%C3%B6nigsberg_%281905%29 A German battleship which was responsible for the sinking of British vessel HMS Pegasus during the Battle of Zanzibar. When she later retreated to the Rufiji Delta in East Africa to repair damage to her engines, the British sent two monitors, Mersey and Severn, to destroy the her – the operation was named the Battle of the Rufiji Delta. On 11 July 1915, the British inflicted sufficient damage to the Königsberg, to force her crew to scuttle the ship. The surviving crew salvaged all ten of her main guns and joined Lieutenant Colonel Paul von Lettow-Vorbeck's guerrilla campaign in East Africa.

3. Dazzle camouflage was the brainchild of marine artist Norman Wilkinson in 1917. The aim was to protect British merchant ships by making it difficult for submarines to accurately assess the shape, course, size and range of vessels. Its efficacy is doubtful but they were often extremely brightly coloured and therefore quite a novel sight. https://www.iwm.org.uk/history/5-facts-about-camouflage-in-the-first-world-war

4. RM Caronia was a British ocean liner, launched on 13 July 1904. She was built for Cunard by John Brown & Co. of Glasgow. She left Liverpool on her maiden voyage to New York on 25 February 1905. A successful 1906 cruise from New York to the Mediterranean led to Caronia's being used for cruising frequently in the coming years.
On 14 April 1912 Caronia sent first ice warning at 09:00 to RMS Titanic reporting "bergs, growlers and field ice"
Caronia was briefly placed on Cunard's Boston service in 1914, but the start of World War I caused her to be requisitioned as an armed merchant cruiser. In 1916, she became a troopship and served in that role for the duration, returning to the Liverpool-New York run after the War.
In 1920 Caronia was converted to burn oil instead of coal.
Her last voyage, from London to New York was on 12 September 1932, after which she was sold to be disassembled. Initially sold to Hughes Bolckow for demolition at Blyth, she was resold, renamed Taiseiyo Maru and sailed to Osaka, where she was scrapped in 1933.

5. The silent movie 'The Fall of a Nation' made in 1916 was an attack on the pacifism of William Jennings Bryan and Henry Ford and a call for American preparedness for war. In it, America is unprepared for an attack by the "European Confederated Army" headed by Germany, which invades America and executes children and war veterans. However, America is saved by a pro-war Congressman who raises an army to defeat the invaders with the support of a suffragette. It was perhaps really a timely piece of Hollywood propaganda.

6 Paul Emil von Lettow-Vorbeck (20 March 1870 – 9 March 1964) was a general in the Imperial German Army and the commander of its forces in the German East Africa campaign. For four years, with a force that never exceeded about 14,000 (3,000 Germans and 11,000 Africans), he held in check a much larger force of 300,000 British, Belgian, and Portuguese troops. Essentially undefeated in the field, von Lettow-Vorbeck was the only German commander to successfully invade imperial British soil during World War I. His exploits in the campaign have come down "as the greatest single guerrilla operation in history, and the most successful."

7 There are records relating to all masonic lodges and, though it provides little information, this is the link to the record regarding Inanda Lodge; *https://www.dhi.ac.uk/lane/record.php?ID=2721*

8 The Gaika – Union Castle Line, built by Harland and Wolff, launched 1897, scrapped 1929
The SS Gaika was a Union Steamship Company vessel built in 1897 by Harland & Wolff at Belfast with a tonnage of 6287 grt, a length of 430ft, a beam of 52ft 2in and a service speed of 12.5 knots. She was used as a troop transporter during the Boer War and transferred to the Union Castle Steamship company in 1900. In WW1 she remained defensively armed on the Africa service but under Government control, her accommodation being mainly used by Civil Servants. She was scrapped in 1928.

9 A Monetary History of German East Africa by John E. Sandrock *http://thecurrencycollector.com/pdfs/A_MONETARY_HISTORY_OF_GERMAN_EAST_AFRICA.pdf*

10 Jon Weier for the Voluntary Action History Society wrote this piece entitles "The YMCA at War" - The full piece can be viewed here: http://www.vahs.org.uk/2013/04/feature-4/

11 Andrew Knighton's blog. General Jan Smuts: Fighting Snobbery and Germany in East Africa in WW1 https://www.warhistoryonline.com/world-war-i/general-jan-smuts-fighting-snobbery-germany-east-africa-world-war-one-m.html

12 Kavirondo was a tugboat built by Bow, McLachlan & Co in 1912 and launched at Kisumu in 1913. During the War, she served as a gunboat. In about 1984, she was laid up at Kisumu and later was used as an accommodation vessel. She later sank alongside, but in 2005 was raised. Her purchasers intended to lengthen and re-engine her for use as a tanker.

13 International Encyclopedia of the First World War. Askaris by Michelle Moyd https://encyclopedia.1914-1918-online.net/article/askari

14 https://encyclopedia.1914-1918-online.net/article/askari
"During and after World War I, the askari of the Schutztruppe gained widespread notoriety for their fighting skills, as well as for their supposed dedication and loyalty to Lettow-Vorbeck, and by extension, to the German Empire. The truth was more complicated. Most askari who remained to the end of the campaign were men who had been members of the Schutztruppe when the war began, and thus viewed it as the protector of their long-term interests. Thousands of others died in the war, became captives or deserted the army, often ending up in the ranks of

the British colonial army in East Africa, the KAR. In particular, in April 1917 the British created the two battalions of the 6 KAR in order to make use of captured ex-German askari........."

15 The Stokes Mortar was invented in 1915 by Frederick Wilfred Scott Stokes in his back garden in Surrey. The British Army needed something to be a match for the German Army's Minenwerfer mortar, which was in use on the Western Front. The Stokes mortar was a simple weapon which could fire as many as 25 bombs per minute and had a maximum range of 800 yards. It was also fairly portable making it ideal for use in the East Africa campaign.

16 The 1918 Spring Offensive or *Kaiserschlacht* (*Kaiser's Battle*), also known as the Ludendorff Offensive, was a series of German attacks along the Western Front during the First World War, beginning on 21 March 1918; https://en.wikipedia.org/wiki/Spring_Offensive

17 The Hotchkiss M1909 (also known as the Hotchkiss Mark I) was a light machine gun of the early 20th century, developed and built by Hotchkiss et Cie. It was based on a design by a Viennese nobleman and Austrian Army officer, Adolf Odkolek von Újezd, who sold the manufacturing rights to Hotchkiss in 1893.

18 This contemporary account of the prevention and management of Malaria during the Great War was taken from the 1916 Manual: "Memoranda on Some Medical Diseases in the Mediterranean War Area with some Sanitary Notes", 1916, Published under the Authority of His Majesty's Stationary Office, London. It is edited by Dr M. Geoffrey Miller, Editor http://vlib.us/medical/malaria.htm

19 The Uganda Journal, Volume 25, Number 1, March 1961.
The Uganda Literary and Scientific Society was established at Entebbe, Uganda Protectorate, in 1923. Its main activity consisted of the reading of papers and the delivery of lectures on topics relating to Uganda. Amongst other things, the journal recorded the history of Uganda and in this volume looked in some detail at the 1918 campaign. https://www.wdl.org/en/item/13805/view/1/29/

20 An extract from How the Great War Razed East Africa – Edward Paice, The Africa Research Institute ....
"*The official death toll among British imperial troops who fought in East Africa was 11,189 – a mortality rate of 9%. No fewer than 95,000 carriers died, bringing the total official death toll of the British war effort to more than 105,000...........The true figures were undoubtedly much higher. As many a British official admitted, "the full tale of mortality among native carriers will never be told".[10] Even 105,000 deaths is a sobering figure. It equals the number of British soldiers killed in the carnage on the Somme between July and November 1916. It is more than 50% higher than the number of Australian or Canadian or Indian troops who gave their lives in the Great War – and whose sacrifice is much more widely recognised. Indeed, the death toll alone in East Africa is comparable to the combined casualties – the dead and wounded – sustained by Indian troops in the Great War.*"

Follow the link to rad the full article. https://www.africaresearchinstitute.org/newsite/publications/how-the-great-war-razed-east-africa/#S8

21 A boma is a livestock enclosure commonly used in the African Great Lakes region. It is incorporated into many African languages, as well as colonial varieties of English, French and German. https://en.wikipedia.org/wiki/Boma_%28enclosure%29

22 Effendi is defined in the OED as - A man of high education or social standing in an eastern Mediterranean or Arab country, so I wonder if this is a term that had migrated to Africa through it's various colonial influences and/or through its proximity (particularly in East Africa) to Arab countries. Colonial forces in East Africa were often built from soldiers originally of the Egyptian army. These units entered East Africa with some officers who brought their title of effendi with them, so it continued to be used for non-European officers in WW1 on both sides.

23 From an article on The British Empire web pages entitled "Nyanza Watering Place - The Remarkable Story of the SS William MacKinnon" by By Ian H Grant   https://www.britishempire.co.uk/article/nyanzawateringplace.htm